Kid Concoctions, Creations & Contraptio

by Robynne Eagan

illustrated by Darcy Tom & Teresa Mathis

Teaching & Learning Company

1204 Buchanan St., P.O. Box 10

Carthage, IL 62321-0010

This book belongs to

____

Kid Concoctions, Creations & Contraptions
is a compilation of three previously published books:
TLC10008 *Kid Concoctions*
TLC10009 *Kid Creations*
TLC10023 *Kid Contraptions*

Cover art by Darcy Tom & Teresa Mathis

ISBN No. 1-57310-455-8

Printing No. 987654321

Teaching & Learning Company
1204 Buchanan St., P.O. Box 10
Carthage, IL 62321-0010

Table of Contents

Dear Teacher or Parent,

Tap into the natural curiosity of young children by turning your teaching environment into an exciting place of learning. This compendium of *Kid Contraptions, Kid Concoctions* and *Kid Creations* is packed with hands-on activities that will encourage students to investigate, create and discover while acquiring knowledge and skill in all areas of the curriculum.

Open-ended learning activities allow students to explore scientific concepts through active experimentation, design technological contraptions that really work and stir up art supplies that will stimulate their senses. Process and content are combined using a variety of instructional approaches devised to develop problem-solving abilities and encourage independent discovery.

Activities are presented in an easy-to-follow format with step-by-step instructions, at-a-glance symbols and concise facts and information. Educators are provided with clear aims and objectives, concept-reinforcing extension activities, reproducible challenges and program assessment tools.

Prepare for action and excitement as you help young learners discover the scientist, inventor and artist within!

Sincerely,

Robynne

Robynne Eagan

Concoctions

Foreword

This section is full of weird and wonderful kid-appealing concoctions for neat stuff to make and do. These concoctions tap into kids' curiosity and natural learning style to enhance skill development and make any curriculum topic more interesting.

Acknowledgements

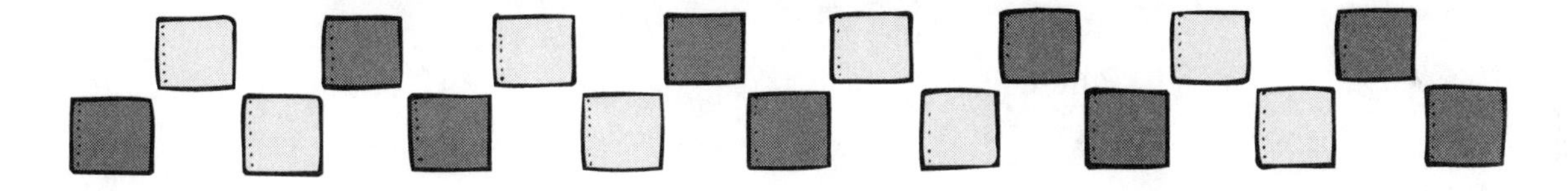

I would like to acknowledge my grandfather "Bertie" Johnson's contribution to this collection. He brought me buckets of sand and pumped basins of water for my first experiments with the physical properties of materials. To Rusty and Dennise Cochrane, recognition for making those first mud pies with me, for pouring and stirring everything we could find in the bathroom sink and for your continued creative suggestions. And thank you to my grandmothers Edith Cochrane and Elizabeth Johnson for allowing us to crack our own eggs and create messes as we experimented and made discoveries over the years.

Thank you to the educators, parents and children who have offered suggestions and who have in some way helped to create the concoctions in this collection. Special appreciation is extended to the educators who taught me and those I have worked with, for helping me to understand that the key to teaching is to excite a child's curiosity.

Table of Contents

Symbol Key

These symbols will provide at-a-glance information regarding the preparation of the mixtures.

K, 1, 2, 3 Recommended grade level

Full child participation in preparation

Partial child participation in preparation

Caution, extra supervision advised

Ten minutes of active preparation time

Ten to sixty minutes of active preparation time

Over one hour of active preparation time

Good group project

Edible

Ingredients may be hard to find

Gift

Large space requirements

Mixture needs cooking. Caution required.

Material will last for one to two weeks

Material will last for one to two months

Material will last for over three months

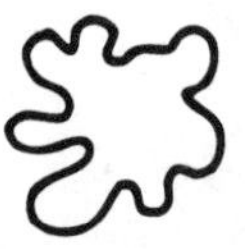
Messy

Measurement Equivalents

These will be useful if you divide recipes into small units to enable greater participation.

1 tablespoon = 3 teaspoons
1/2 tablespoon = 1 1/2 teaspoons
4 tablespoons = 1/4 cup
5 tablespoons and 1 teaspoon = 1/3 cup

Metric Conversions:

1 dry ounce = 28 grams
1 dry pound = 373 grams
1 liquid ounce = 29.5 milliliters
1 cup = .24 liter
1 pint = .47 liter
1 quart = .95 liter
1 gallon = 3.8 liters

1 cup = 250 milliliters
1/2 cup = 125 milliliters
1 teaspoon = 5 milliliters
1 tablespoon = 15 milliliters
1/4 cup = 60 milliliters
1 inch = 2.54 centimeters
1/4-inch thickness = 5 millimeters thickness

Oven Temperatures:

250°F = 123°C
275°F = 135°C
325°F = 163°C
350°F = 177°C
375°F = 191°C
400°F = 204°C

Guidelines to Facilitate Creative Learning

1. Respect a child's right to explore. Provide materials, resources and stimulating ideas that will lead children to their own questions and discoveries.

2. Introduce skills, techniques and information in response to a child's curiosity and needs.

3. Organize. Have clear aims and objectives in mind. Read instructions, have materials ready and go through a trial run. Children should be able to experiment and make discoveries with little assistance.

4. Be flexible. Students may not make the discoveries you expect.

5. Learn to recognize and praise children's skills of problem solving, questioning, observation, analysis and discovery.

6. Promote children's confidence in their own abilities.

7. Evaluate the child's progress through observation of many experiences. Offer positive comments on the processes mastered and the concepts grasped.

8. Prepare for some degree of mess. Encourage students to participate in the planning and cleaning of a creative learning environment suitable to everyone involved.

Rainbow Potion

K-3  

Materials:

jar
1 ounce (29.57 ml) cup
small fork
1 T (15 ml) cooking oil
4 drops each of red, blue and green food coloring
water

Process:

1. Fill the jar with water.
2. Pour cooking oil into the cup.
3. Add 4 drops of each of the food coloring colors.
4. Beat the oil and colors with a fork until thoroughly mixed.
5. Pour the mixture of oil and food coloring into the water.
6. Keep the jar still and observe for 5 to 10 minutes.

Try This:

- Set this up as a center. Allow children to explore with the oil, water and colors.
- What happens when this mixture is stirred up?
- Encourage students to observe and discuss what they see.
- Small pools of oil spotted with tiny spheres of color float on the surface of the water. Individual spheres of color appear to explode outward, producing flat circles of color on the surface of the water with streams of color that sink down through the water. Food coloring is water-based, and oil and water do not mix.

Mud Pie

A favorite old classic.

Materials:

sand
clean dirt
water (as needed)
cake pan or pie plate
tiny stones, sand, leaves, grass, wildflowers, seeds
sunshine
large bowl or pail

Process:

1. Mix clean sand, dirt and some water with your hands in the large bowl or pail.
2. Add more water as needed, but keep the mixture really thick.
3. Line a cake pan or pie plate with grass to prevent sticking.
4. Pour the mixture into the pan.
5. Sprinkle on a layer of tiny stones; dry, white sand; or plant material.
6. Add another layer of mud.
7. Decorate with flower petals, leaves, seeds or black mud "icing."
8. Bake in the sun until ready "to serve"!

Try This:

- Have a "bake off" and allow all students to be "judges" choosing the best pie. (You may want to establish several categories so there will be many winners.)
- Encourage creative decorating techniques for this outdoor art class.
- Incorporate with a math activity. Make play money and have students buy and sell pies at the bake shop.
- Have students follow up with a written recipe or a story about the pie.
- Speed up the "cooking" process up by putting in a warm oven 150°F (65°C) until the pie starts to crack slightly on the surface. The cooking time will vary according to the size and moisture content of the pie.

Musical Vegetables

2-3  

Caution

Materials:

gourd or squash
pointy object (hammer and nail)*

Process:

1. Make some holes into a gourd or squash using a hammer and nail.
2. Leave the gourd or squash to dry for one month.
3. Turn the holey gourd or squash every other day.
4. In one month shake it up, and you will have a maraca.

Try This:

- Have every student make a maraca. Use this as a steppingstone to creating a class band. Other instruments can be made to complement the maraca band.
- Incorporate the turning of the maracas into the class calendar. Students can use their pattern skills to recognize what days the maracas need to be turned. (Try to start this activity at the beginning of a month.)
- If students have a building center, allow them to use the hammer and nail–punch the holes ahead of time for the sake of safety.
- Integrate this activity with a harvest unit.

* Caution: Be careful using hammer and nail.

Wishing Dust

A wonderful way to finish off a school barbecue or campfire.

Materials:

campfire (or charcoal barbecue)
sugar
glitter (optional)
a wish

Process:

1. At the end of a barbecue or campfire sing-along, have children think of a wish.

2. Distribute handfuls (about 1 ounce each) of wishing dust.

3. Children whisper their wish into the dust and keep their hands closed.

4. With adult supervision, each child throws his handful of wishing dust and wish into the fire. The fire will flare brightly and sometimes with color to demonstrate that "the wish was received."

Try This:

- Depending upon the time of year, this may be a special holiday wish, a wish for the summer holiday or a wish for the new school year.

Pasta Colors

K-2  

Materials:

large clear plastic bag
3 drops of food coloring
2 T (30 ml) water
1 package of pasta
tray

Process:

1. Pour uncooked pasta shapes into bag.
2. Add food coloring and water.
3. Shake until the pasta appears well colored.
4. Spread pasta on tray to air dry.
5. When dry, use or store in sealed container for later use.

Try This:

- There are many interesting pasta shapes on the market and various food colors available, allowing for many variations.
- Use as a manipulative for hands-on math programs–it is perfect for sorting and classifying activities. Section off a paper plate and sort away!
- Use for various art and craft activities. Try a pasta collage, a pasta rainbow, a mosaic, thread pasta on a string for jewelry and make a pasta dinner glued to the plate.
- Pasta alphabets can be used for colorful greetings and messages.
- Kids love learning the interesting pasta names. Use these names and record them on a chart for a lesson in letter sounds.

Pasta Creatures

K-3  

Materials:

1 cup (250 ml) of tiny pasta pieces per child (pasta letters or pastina works well)
3 T (45 ml) or more of water for each cup of pasta
food coloring (optional)
large pot or bowl
wooden spoon

Process:

1. Pour the desired amount of pasta into a large pot or bowl.
2. Add food coloring to water if color is desired.
3. Add the water, a little at a time, and stir until the pasta has a sticky, clay-like consistency.
4. Form the pasta mixture into sculptures.
5. Let the sculptures dry thoroughly until they are hard.

Try This:

- Bend a paper clip into a hanging hook. Gently poke one end of the paper clip into the top of the wet sculpture. When it dries, the sculpture can be hung in a place of honor.
- When the sculpture has thoroughly dried, it can be painted.
- Make a sculpture of a snowy village using this material–add some glitter and white paint.

Pouring Plastic

2-3  

Materials:

1 envelope unflavored gelatin
3 T (45 ml) water
3 drops food coloring
cookie cutters or molds
saucepan
spoon
stove

Process:

1. Add gelatin and water to pot.
2. Add enough food coloring to give you the shade you desire.
3. Cook over medium heat, stirring constantly until everything dissolves and blends together.
4. Pour the mixture into metal cookie cutters or molds.
5. Let dry until the edges are hard and sharp–about 24 hours.
6. When the creations are dry, remove them from their molds.

Try This:

- Pour a thin layer of plastic onto a cookie sheet. Students can cut shapes from this or use a paper punch to punch lots of plastic sequins for later creations.
- Punch holes in creations to thread string through for hanging.
- For broaches and buttons, put pins on the wet plastic to harden.

Water Sculptures

K-3  

Materials:

water
interesting containers: molds, milk cartons, tin cans, plastic jugs and cups
food coloring
cold weather (below 32°F [0°C])

Process:

1. Round up some interesting containers. Use old cake pans, jelly molds, plastic containers and tin cans. Cardboard milk cartons are perfect for making building blocks.
2. If you want colored blocks, add food coloring to the water.
3. Pour water into the containers and freeze outside until completely hard.
4. Pop the ice blocks out of their containers as they freeze and make more.
5. Place the shapes in the shade so they will last longer.
6. Build, create, carve and paint your ice structures.

Try This:

- Involve the entire class in the planning and building of the ultimate ice fort or more ambitious ice castle. Have students draw up plans, assign tasks and collect containers.
- Sculptures can be created by chipping and carving with blunt tools or by melting and warming with your hands or warm water.
- Incorporate this activity into a unit on winter.
- Include this activity in a school winter carnival.

Mud Fossils

1-3   

Materials:

soil
water
cookie sheet
bowl
spoon
small items: shells, leaves, wood, pebbles, coins, keys

Process:

1. Fill a container half full with soil. Soil with clay in it will work best. Squeeze the soil in your hand–if it adheres together well and forms a ball, it will work.
2. Mix water with soil until the mixture is thick and hand-moldable.
3. Stir in little items such as shells, pebbles, coins, keys or other washable items.
4. Completely conceal the items in the mud.
5. Allow mud to dry for at least 24 hours.
6. Break the mud open with your hands and remove the hidden objects.
7. Now look for the homemade fossils.

Try This:

- Integrate this activity into a study of fossils. After this activity, students will better understand how fossils were formed and what they are.
- Integrate this activity with a unit on dinosaurs.
- Do rubbings of the fossil.
- Make a plaster casting of a fossil by pouring plaster into the impression and letting it dry.
- Take students on a fossil hunt or to a museum to study fossils.
- Treat the activity as an art activity–put a lot of time into planning the layout of the fossil.
- Variation: Use plaster of Paris in place of the mud and have students chip away at the plaster using blunt instruments.

Magic Copper Cleaner

K-3  

Materials:

1 cup (250 ml) white vinegar
1/4 cup (60 ml) table salt
bowl
spoon
copper pennies, buttons, cups, jewelry or other items

Process:

1. Pour vinegar into the bowl.
2. Add salt and stir until the solution is clear.
3. Add tarnished items to the bowl and stir gently. The copper pieces will change before your eyes!

Try This:

- Throw hundreds of pennies into the school yard and have children go on a treasure hunt. Stir the pennies into the magic solution and watch in awe. Follow up with math activities using the bright, shiny coppers.

Help Save the Earth Concoctions

K-3   

Environment friendly, practical concoctions kids can feel good about.

Materials:

clean containers with sealing lids
labels
funnels for pouring
See options below.

Wonder Cleaner

Materials:

white distilled vinegar

Process:

1. Pour vinegar into container (a squirt bottle of some sort would be best for this cleaner).

2. Affix label that reads:
   Wonder Cleaner works wonders removing stains, mold, grease and odors. It adds sparkle and shine to windows, mirrors, all glass, paintbrushes and floors. It can add softness to your wash if added in the rinse cycle.

Pure Clean

K-3  

Materials:

pure soap (can be purchased in grocery or hardware stores in flakes, powder, bars or liquid form)
containers
labels

Process:

1. Put soap into appropriate container for the soap form you are using.
2. Affix a label that reads:
   Keep the environment clean while you clean with Pure Clean. Clean up those clothes, dishes, floors, toys or even your car.

Clean Air

K-3   

Materials:

white distilled vinegar
containers with lids
labels

Process:

1. Decorate a container with a tight-sealing lid.

2. Fill the container with vinegar.

3. Add a label that reads:
   Clean Air will absorb odors you don't want around. Remove the lid and let Clean Air start working for your air. Pour into a fancy bowl for a special occasion or place on your stove to warm Clean Air and make it work even harder.

Try This:

- Turn your classroom into a manufacturing plant. Provide students with the information and materials they need to develop product names, design logos, create slogans and package their products. Incorporate this project with a study of manufacturing, advertising and marketing. Help kids to recognize marketing schemes aimed at them.
- Encourage students to think about the products and packaging they consume. Look at the effects various items have on the environment.
- They act as natural air cleaners, filtering common indoor air pollutants such as formaldehyde, benzene and tricholorethylene. Aloe vera plant, spider plant, pot mum, golden pathos, peace lily and English ivy act as natural air cleaners. This task could be incorporated into a study of plants, gardening, the environment or pollution.
- These "gifts to the Earth" can be made as gifts for various occasions or can be sold at a school fund-raising event.

Chapter 2

Bubble Brews

Bubbles, amazing bubbles. Easy to make. A wonder to watch. They float and swirl and disappear or burst before your eyes.

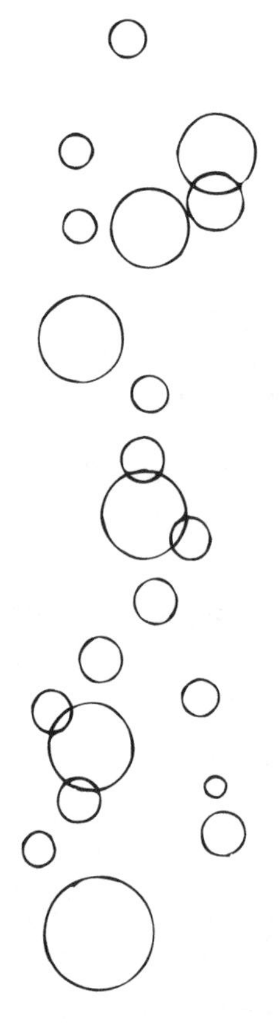

- Good Bubble Weather–The best bubbles are made on cool days, with high humidity and no wind. Bubbles last longer when there is water in the air. Early evenings, night and early mornings are usually good times for bubbling.

- The best surface for bubble making is a paved, nonslip surface–like a school yard. A group of children and their bubble brews might be more suds than the school lawn can handle.

- Bend thin coat hangers or pipe cleaners into loops for bubble blowers.

- To make enormous bubbles, dip the large end of a plastic kitchen funnel into the solution and blow through the small end.

- Joy™ or Dawn™ commercial dish soaps work best for bubbles.

- The longer your solution sits, the better it gets.

- Experiment with common objects as bubble blowers. How about a straw or a key ring? Have students bring in as many potential bubble-blowing devices as they can find.

Small Blower

K-3  

Materials:

thin wire
scissors or wire cutter
duct tape

Process:

1. Cut wire about 5" to 7" (12.7 to 17.78 cm) long.
2. Bend the wire to make a loop.
3. Twist the end of the wire around the handle and tape.
4. Pour bubble brew into a small container about 3" (7.62 cm) deep.
5. Dip the loop into your brew and blow gently on the film in the hole or wave it through the air.

Try This:

- Bend your loop into different shapes.

Hoop Blower

Materials:

wire clothes hanger
pliers
duct tape
3 feet (.91 m) of yarn

Process:

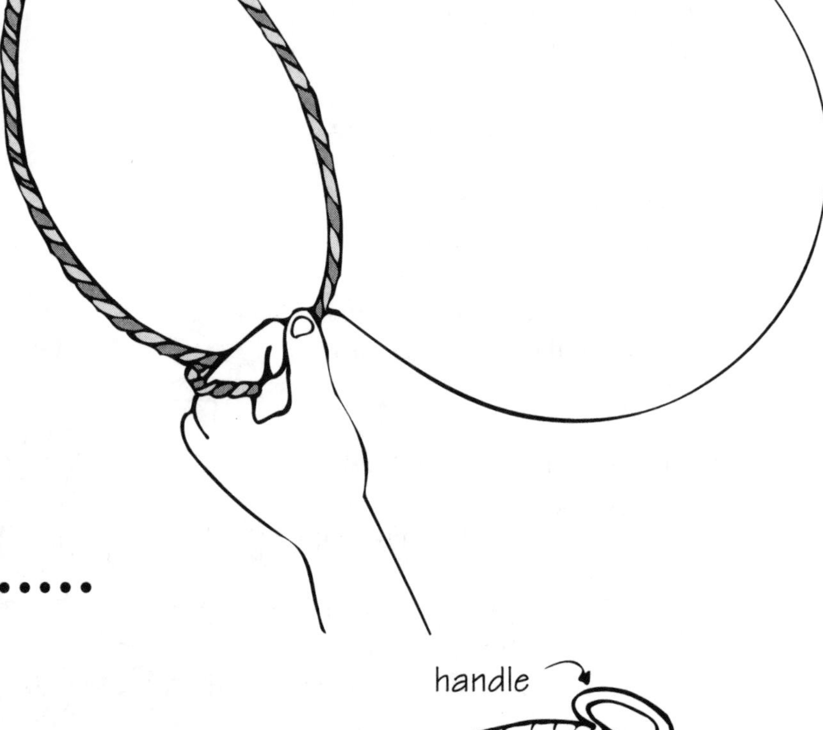

1. Bend the wire hanger into a circle. Use pliers to add an extra twist or two to make the hoop smaller.
2. Wrap the hoop with tape so it is safe–this will be your handle.
3. Wrap yarn around the hoop. The yarn will soak up the soap and grip the soap film.
4. Dip the hoop and pull it out.

Try This:

- Try to catch a small bubble inside a large one. Form the large bubble around the small one.

handle

clothes hanger

yarn wrapped around

Bubble Brew

K-3  

Materials:

1 quart (.95 l) water
2-quart (1.9 l) bottle with a tight lid
4 ounces (118.28 ml) liquid dishwashing soap or detergent
measuring cup
3 T (45 ml) glycerine (available at drugstores)
bowl

Process:

1. Put the water into the bottle.
2. Add dishwashing soap.
3. Add the glycerine.
4. Put the lid on the bottle and shake it up.
5. Let the mixture sit in a warm place for about 30 minutes.

Try This:

- If you see froth in the solution, clear it away with a dry finger, or it will interfere with the film needed for large soap bubbles.
- Make the Best Brew Center. Have students stir up their own brews to find the right combination of ingredients. This will take a lot of group interaction, experimentation, recording and problem solving.

Super Giant Bubbles

K-3  

Bubbles beyond belief!

Materials:

3/4 cup (180 ml) cold clear water
1 T (15 ml) sugar
1/4 cup (60 ml) clear liquid dish soap
1/4 cup (60 ml) glycerine (available at drugstores)
large flat dish or pan
bubble hoop

Process:

1. Stir water and sugar together.
2. Add glycerine and soap.
3. Let sit for 20 minutes.
4. Stir well and pour into a large flat container for making your bubbles.

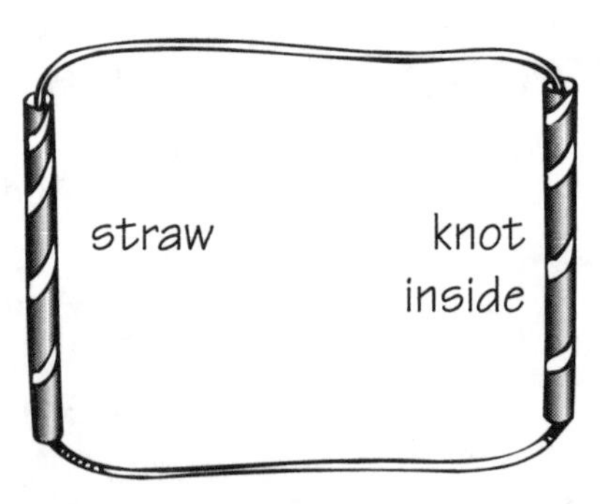

Try This:

- Add more glycerine to make the bubbles even stronger.
- Dip the hoop into the solution then wave it in the air.
- Try using a straw-and-yarn bubble maker. Thread a 2 1/2 foot (.76 m) length of string through two straws. Tie the ends together. Dip your straw-and-yarn bubble maker into the solution. Lift out by the straws.
- Make a soap film floor to bounce other bubbles on or wave it through the air and flip your wrist a little to set the bubble free. Is your bubble square? Can you trap a smaller bubble inside as you wave and flip?

Frozen Bubbles

K-3  

A cool activity with great results.

Materials:

bubble solution

bubble blower

cold weather

Process:

1. Blow some bubbles on a calm wintry day when the temperature is below 32ºF (0ºC). On a very cold day bubbles freeze almost instantly.
2. Blow your bubble inside, catch it and take it out. The bubble will freeze. Watch the frozen spot grow until the bubble breaks because it has lost its elasticity.
3. Watch the frozen section float off into the winter day.

Try This:

- Try poking a hole in the bubble before it breaks. If you are really tricky, you might be able to blow a smaller bubble into the hole!
- Some people have reported blowing bubbles that don't break when they freeze. Try your hand at it.

Bubbly Soda

K-3  

Tiny bubbles that will amaze you.

Materials:

small jar
4 ounces (118.28 ml) soda pop
1 tsp of salt

Process:

1. Fill a small container half full of soda pop.
2. Add salt.
3. Observe as bubbles form and then rise to the top.

Try This:

- Introduce the scientific method of investigation. Have students write up this simple experiment.
- Add a peanut to the jar.

Bubble Art

K-3  

Materials:

paint shirts
tablecloth
flat pan
1 cup (250 ml) water
3 T (45 ml) liquid tempera paint
1 T (15 ml) dishwashing detergent
straws
paper

Process:

1. Cover children's clothing with paint shirts and cover the work surface with a plastic tablecloth.

2. Pour the water, paint and detergent into bowl or pan.

3. Children will bring their straws to the mixture, put one end in and blow. Practice blowing before the straw goes in. Ensure children know the difference between blowing out and sucking in!

4. Blow and blow until the bubbles are bubbling out of the container.

5. Gently place the paper over the top of the bowl, allowing the paper to touch the bubbles.

6. Remove the paper and allow it to dry. "Bubble up" for the next paper.

Try This:

- Provide groups with the ingredients to make their own bowl of bubbles–each in a different color. Allow experimentation with varying amounts of paint. Children can rotate from group to group creating colorful bubble pictures.
- When the papers have dried, cut them into the shape of bubbles for a bubbly display. Students can write bubble poems on these bubbles.
- Shape the bubble art into fans for a wonderful effect.

* Caution: *Blow* through the straw!

Purple Volcano

K-3  

Tiny bubbles with a colorful twist!

Materials:

1 tall, skinny glass
4 ounces (118.28 ml) purple grape juice (must be real grape juice)
4 tsp (20 ml) baking soda
4 tsp (20 ml) white vinegar

Process:

1. Fill the glass half full with grape juice.

2. Stir in a small spoonful of baking soda.

3. Watch for amazing results.

4. Now add 1 teaspoon (5 ml) of white vinegar and look for the foam and color change again. Continue alternating vinegar and soda for bubbly, colorful fun.

Try This:

- The carbon dioxide bubbles are by-products of the combination of vinegar and baking soda. The grape juice helps us see those bubbles.
- Set up a science table where students can experiment with various combinations. With a little soap, vinegar, water, baking soda, food coloring and soda pop, you will set the stage for safe bubbly fun.

Bubble Up

K-3  

Materials:

glass
2 ounces (59.14 ml) white vinegar
3 seashells

Process:

1. Pour vinegar into a glass.
2. Add the seashells.
3. If there is limestone in the shells, you'll have your very own bubble factory!

Try This:

- Bubble Center: Provide students with a vinegar bath and an assortment of items. Have students predict which ones will produce bubbles when set in the bath. Can students explain why some do and some don't?

Bubble Power

K-3  

Materials:

1 tsp (5 ml) active dry yeast
1/4 cup (60 ml) sugar
1 cup (250 ml) warm water
1 small balloon with a neck that will stretch over the top of the bottle
1 quart (.95 l) soda pop bottle
funnel
bowl

Process:

1. Blow the balloon up and then let the air out to "stretch" it.

2. Combine the sugar, the yeast and the water in the bottle. You might need the funnel.

3. Hold your hand over the bottle opening and shake to mix it all up.

4. Fit the balloon over the opening in the bottle.

5. Set the bottle into a bowl filled with almost-hot water.

6. Let it sit for about 1 hour.

7. Observe.

Try This:

- Before the task, ask students what will happen. Record their guesses.
- After the project, ask students why they think this happened.
- The yeast fed on the sugar and produced carbon dioxide which filled the balloon. Have students look for little holes in a loaf of bread or a cake.
- Try this with 1/4 cup (60 ml) vinegar in the bottle and 2 T (30 ml) of baking soda in the balloon–no bowl of warm water needed. When the balloon is fitted on the bottle and the soda meets the vinegar, carbon dioxide is released and the balloon fills up.
- Discuss other forms of gases.

Rainbow Crystal Garden

2-3  

* Caution

Fascinating!

Materials:

2 charcoal briquettes
6 T (90 ml) iodized salt
1 T (15 ml) household ammonia
6 T (90 ml) laundry bluing
6 T (90 ml) water
throwaway aluminum pie tin
food coloring
container

Process:

1. In a container, mix together 1 or 2 tablespoons (15 or 30 ml) each of liquid bluing, iodized salt and ammonia and water.

2. Stir to dissolve as much salt as possible.

3. Break the charcoal into chunks and place into the disposable pie tin.

4. Add a few drops of food coloring to each piece.

5. Pour the liquid solution over top of charcoal pieces.

6. Within an hour, frosty formations will begin to appear and will continue to grow almost indefinitely.

7. Add more liquid solution as it evaporates.

8. Admire the beautiful colors and shapes carefully. The crystal formations are so fragile that even a little bump of the table will cause them to crumble.

Try This:

- For the sake of safety, do this activity ahead of time and let your class see the results.
- Give students materials to sketch the crystal formations they see.
- Give students various colors of paint to try to re-create the beautiful colors.

* Caution: Be careful when handling ammonia. Use materials in a well-ventilated area and have students stand a safe distance away.

Crystals and Needles

K-3  

Materials:

4 T (60 ml) Epsom salts
1 cup (250 ml) water
measuring cup
black construction paper
scissors
lid from a large jar

Process:

1. Cut a circle from black paper that will fit inside the lid.
2. Place the paper in the lid.
3. Add 4 tablespoons (60 ml) Epsom salts to the water in the measuring cup and stir until clear.
4. Pour a very thin layer of the mixture into the lid.
5. Let stand undisturbed for 24 hours.

Long needle-shaped crystals will form on the black paper as the water evaporates.

Try This:

- Find out why the crystals formed. Ask students to speculate.
- When the water evaporated, it left the salts which arranged themselves into a crystal pattern. Sugar, salt and other substances form their own particular type of pattern. Have students compare the patterns from the various projects.
- Lead a "crystal hike." Students take pencil and paper and record things that look like crystal patterns around the school and school yard.
- Many art activities can arise from the study of crystal formations. Have students create their own patterns with various artistic media.

Salty Crystals

K-3  

Materials:

1/2 cup (125 ml) water
1/4 cup (60 ml) salt
bowl
spoon

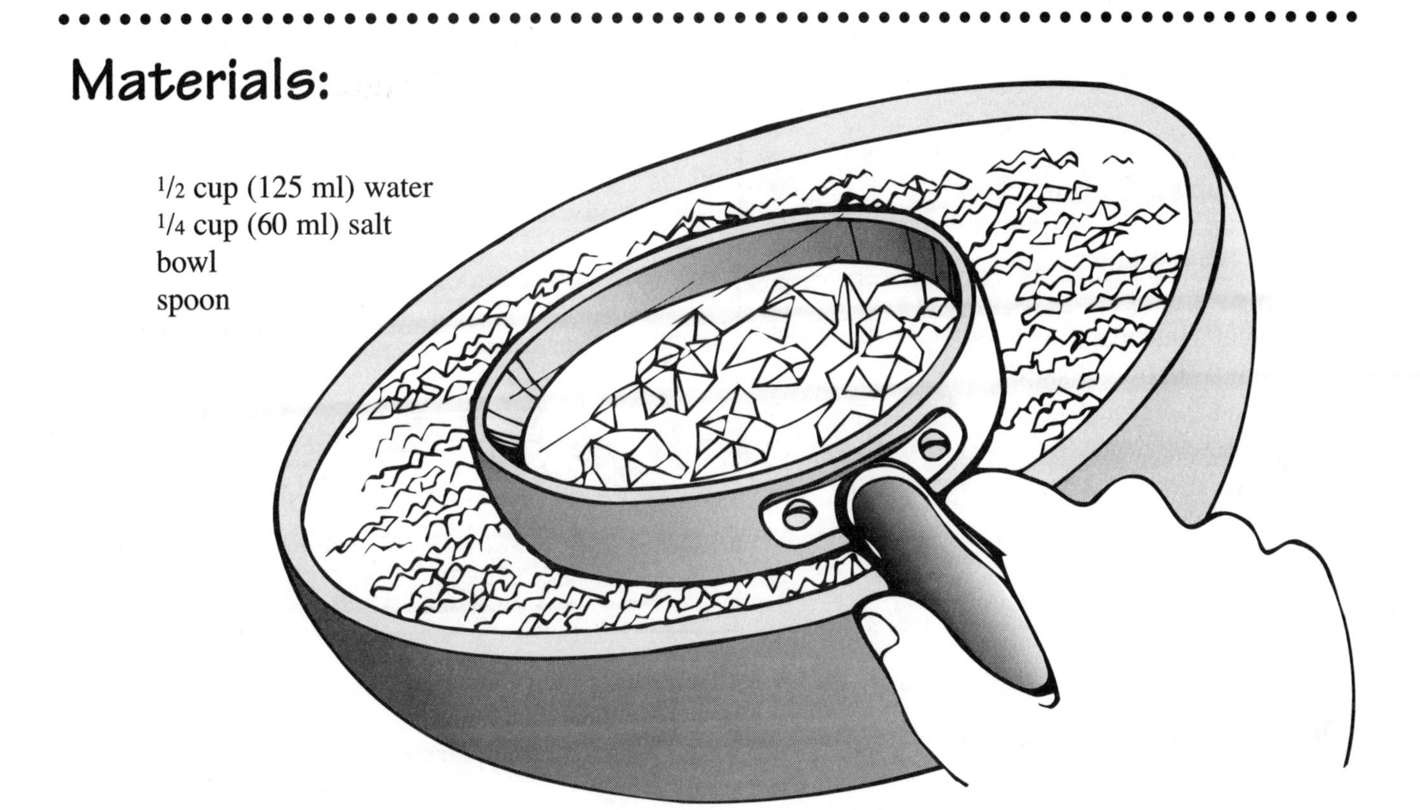

Process:

1. Stir the water and salt together in a bowl.
2. Allow the bowl to sit undisturbed in a warm place until all the water evaporates (3 to 4 weeks).
3. Slow evaporation of the water leaves behind clear cubic salt crystals called halite.

Try This:

- Put one bowl of this solution in a cool place and one in a warm place. What differences are observed? Are there any theories to explain the differences?
- Look at the crystals through a magnifying glass.

Candy on a String

K-3  

Recovering solute crystals–an experiment you can eat.

Materials:

1/2 cup (125 ml) water
1 cup (250 ml) granulated sugar
wooden spoon
measuring cup
small saucepan
small shallow dishes
stove
string
craft stick

Process:

1. Stir water and a spoonful of sugar in the pan over low heat.
2. Add spoonfuls of sugar, one at a time, stirring each addition until it dissolves.
3. Continue heating gently until all sugar is dissolved.
4. Boil for 1 minute until the solution is thick and clear with no crystals.
5. Pour hot solution into dishes.
6. Let stand.
7. Tie one end of the string to a craft stick.
8. Lay a string in the center of the dish. The sugar crystals will form on it.

Try This:

- Observe the crystalization process with a magnifying glass.
- Look at sugar with a magnifying glass and then with a microscope.
- Encourage students to observe and discuss what they see happening.

Chapter 4

Gruesome Goodies

Everyone loves to hate the sight and feel of creepy things. Offer disgusting, educational fun to teach *and delight* students.

- Haunted tales add extra pizzazz to these gruesome goodies! Try some creative (not too scary) storytelling.

Slime

K-3  

A gross' em out recipe.

Materials:

1 cup (250 ml) cornstarch
1 cup (250 ml) water (You might not need it all.)
green food coloring
square pan or basin
spoon
plastic table cover

Process:

1. Add food coloring to water.
2. Pour 1/2 cup (125 ml) of cornstarch into a bowl.
3. Add water, a few drops at a time and stir.
4. Continue adding water and cornstarch until the mixture seems to become a thick liquid.
5. Use your hands to combine the ingredients when it gets tough to stir.
6. Explore this stuff!
7. When you are through with your slime, let it dry in the pan overnight and then scrape into the garbage.

Try This:

- Pat the mixture with the palm of your hand. Slap it. Try to pick it up. Hold it; pat it; stroke it. Is it wet or dry? Is it a solid or a liquid? It seems like a solid, but it feels slimy!
- Lead a discussion: Is it a liquid or a solid? Discuss properties of both.
- Use this concoction to stimulate language development. Encourage kids to talk about how it feels, how they feel touching it and what it reminds them of. Make a list of adjectives to describe it. Have students write a story about it.
- The grains of starch are packed together but spaced evenly apart. Slow movement allows the grains to keep their spacing and slide past one another like a liquid. Quick movement or pressure jams the grains together making it act like a solid.
- The slime teaches us a lesson in patience. If you approach life with thought and patience, you will get through anything–if you barge through without thinking, you may have a harder time and end up in a mess! Challenge students to tell or write a fable based on this mixture.

Mold Garden

K-3  

What better garden could there be for Halloween?

Materials:

1 slice of white bread with no preservatives
paper napkin
small dish
water
clear plastic bag with ventilation holes

Process:

1. Soak the napkin and place it on the dish.
2. Put the bread on the napkin in the dish.
3. Moisten the bread with a few drops of water.
4. Slip the bread into the plastic bag.
5. Let it sit in a dark place for four or more days.

Try This:

- Look at the bread every day. Record any findings.
- Look at the bread with a microscope or magnifying glass. You should be able to see groups of tiny microscopic organisms called molds. Although these molds are in the air and on surfaces all round us, we only see them when they grow in great numbers as they do in the environment created on the bread.

Recipe for a Haunted House

1-3  

Materials:

blindfolds
unbreakable containers
cooked spaghetti
peeled grapes
peanut butter
frozen gelatin
slime (See page 40.)
soapy water
plastic bugs
gauze strips
chestnuts in pods
wintergreen LifeSavers™

Process:

1. Invite students to your haunted house.
2. Blindfold each one and have them feel the contents of the bowls as you explain what each article is.
3. Set up bowls with the following items in them. For some gruesome fun, suggest what each item could be.

cooked spaghetti
brains
peeled grapes
eyes
slime
bats' blood
frozen gelatin
poison ooze
soapy water with plastic bugs
goblin's stew
gauze strips
spider's web
chestnuts in pods
fighting spiders
wintergreen LifeSavers™
ghostly glowing candy
(crunch one in the dark and see!)
rotting matter
peanut butter

Try This:

- Encourage kids to create their own haunted house in the classroom. Allow students to think up the ghoulish goodies and offer them to the class.
- Incorporate with a discussion of the senses and of textures.

Creepy Clay

K-3  

Materials:

1/2 cup (125 ml) white glue
1 1/2 cups (375 ml) distilled water
1 tsp (5 ml) borax powder
food coloring
2 small bowls
spoon

Process:

1. Stir glue and 1/2 cup (125 ml) water in the small bowl.
2. Add drops of coloring until you get just the right shade–green is gruesome.
3. In the other bowl combine borax with 1 cup (250 ml) of water.
4. Stir until the borax is completely dissolved.
5. Stir the borax mixture constantly while adding the glue mixture a little at a time.
6. Carefully dump the blob of clay onto a flat surface.
7. Knead until smooth and pliable.
8. Squeeze it; bounce it; stretch it; sculpt it. Explore!
9. Store in a covered container for up to one week.

Try This:

- Ask students to describe the feel of this rubbery clay. Use a flip chart to record their adjectives.

* Caution: Be careful using borax powder.

Rubber Egg

K-3  

Kids will love to hate the look and feel of this egg!

Materials:

egg
wide-mouthed jar
white vinegar

Process:

1. Place the egg in the jar and fill it three-fourths full of vinegar.

2. Leave it for three days.

3. Take it out of the vinegar and discover a new sensation. The egg will have lost its hard shell and have only a membrane. It is quite durable in this form, but use a drop cloth or observe and feel it outdoors!

Try This:

- Encourage students to touch and describe this egg.

Bendy Bones

K-3  

Materials:

chicken or turkey bones
1 quart (1 liter) of vinegar
large jar

Process:

1. Clean bones thoroughly. (They can be boiled or scrubbed.)
2. Dry the bones for two days.
3. Put the bones into a jar and cover them with vinegar. This removes the calcium from the bones.
4. Let stand until the bones are bendable–about seven days–depending on the size of the bone.
5. Remove the bones. They won't rattle, but they will bend!

Try This:

- Incorporate with a study of the skeletal system. Minerals make our bones strong and hard. The vinegar removes the minerals from the bone in this experiment.
- Use these bendy bones for some Halloween fun.
- Boil the bones from an entire chicken or turkey and glue them onto thick paper in creative skeletal formations for a dinosaur or Halloween unit.

Chapter 5

Critter Treats

We all love to watch the critters. Set out these treats and sit back and enjoy the wildlife.

- You can make bird feeders from plastic containers, plastic bottles, old milk cartons and if you are ambitious–wood. Hang your feeder in a sheltered place safe from climbing cats or squirrels.
- If you put out a feeder, birds will come to count on that food for their winter survival.
- Fill your feeder right after a snowstorm when the birds will need the food most.

Food Preferences of Common Birds

small to medium seeds:	sparrows, mourning doves, meadowlarks, orioles, red-winged blackbirds
large seeds:	cardinals, blue jays
black oil sunflower seed:	cardinals, chickadees, titmice, grosbeaks, finches, downy woodpeckers, orioles
striped sunflower:	titmice, cardinals, jays, grosbeaks
millet:	doves and sparrows
niger thistle:	finches
hulled sunflower:	finches, jays, cardinals, chickadees
safflower:	cardinals, doves, sparrows
corn:	sparrows, jays, doves, downy woodpeckers
fruit:	catbirds, orioles, redwings, robins, tanagers
large berries (holly, juniper):	cardinals, blue jays, robins
earthworms:	robins
crawling insects:	towhees, killdeer, robins, nuthatches
flying insects:	swallows, house wrens, bluebirds, meadowlarks, red-winged blackbirds
suet:	white-breasted nuthatches, black-capped chickadees
nectar:	hummingbirds, orioles

Bird Bread

K-3  

Materials:

stale bread, doughnuts or unsalted pretzels
cookie cutters, knife or scissors
peanut butter or lard
tray
yarn or string
birdseed

Process:

1. Cut bread with cookie cutters, or use doughnuts or pretzels. Let them go stale.

2. Spread bread, doughnuts or pretzel with peanut butter then press into a tray of birdseed.

3. Hang the edible ornaments from a tree with yarn or string. Take care not to use nylon or plastic as birds may use these for nesting materials.

Try This:

- Hang a diary, a pair of binoculars and a bird identification book or chart by the window. Bird-watchers record their sightings. Record things like the exact spot the bird is seen, what it is doing, how big it is, what shape it is, its color and markings and if a call is heard.
- Birds are generally looking for food or a mate. Students can record in their Bird-Watching Diary what they think the bird is doing.

Scoop and Fill Bird Stations

K-3 

Materials:

half of an orange or grapefruit
suet
birdseed

Process:

1. Scoop out an orange or grapefruit.
2. Fill it halfway with suet and birdseed and place in crook of a tree branch where you can observe the birds.

Try This:

- Variation: Saw coconut shells in half and drill holes. Have students thread string through holes to make this shell feeder hang. Fill with seed and other goodies.

Bird Strings

K-3  

Materials:

edible berries (cranberries, strawberries, blueberries)
peanuts in their shells
apple slices
popped corn
heavy cotton thread
needle
heavy string

Process:

1. Double the thread and thread the needle.
2. String any variation of berries, apple slices, peanuts and popcorn.
3. Hang this string feeder on a tree where you can watch the birds and enjoy.

Try This:

- Use the school Christmas tree for a bird feeder and bird shelter. Stand it in a snowbank and hang your bird feeder on it. It makes a lovely Christmas gift to the birds. Do this the day before Christmas break.

Bird Cones

K-3  

Materials:

string or yarn
large pinecones
peanut butter or suet
birdseed

Process:

1. Tie a string or piece of bright yarn to a large pinecone.
2. Spread the pinecone with peanut butter and roll it in birdseed.
3. Hang it on a tree outside the classroom window or let students take home to hang.

Try This:

- Have plastic bags handy if students will be taking this project home.
- Hang these cones, along with other bird foods, in the discarded Christmas tree.
- Incorporate this with a theme on nutrition. All living things need the right foods to survive and keep healthy.

Hummer Food

1-3 

It's for the *humming*birds!

Materials:

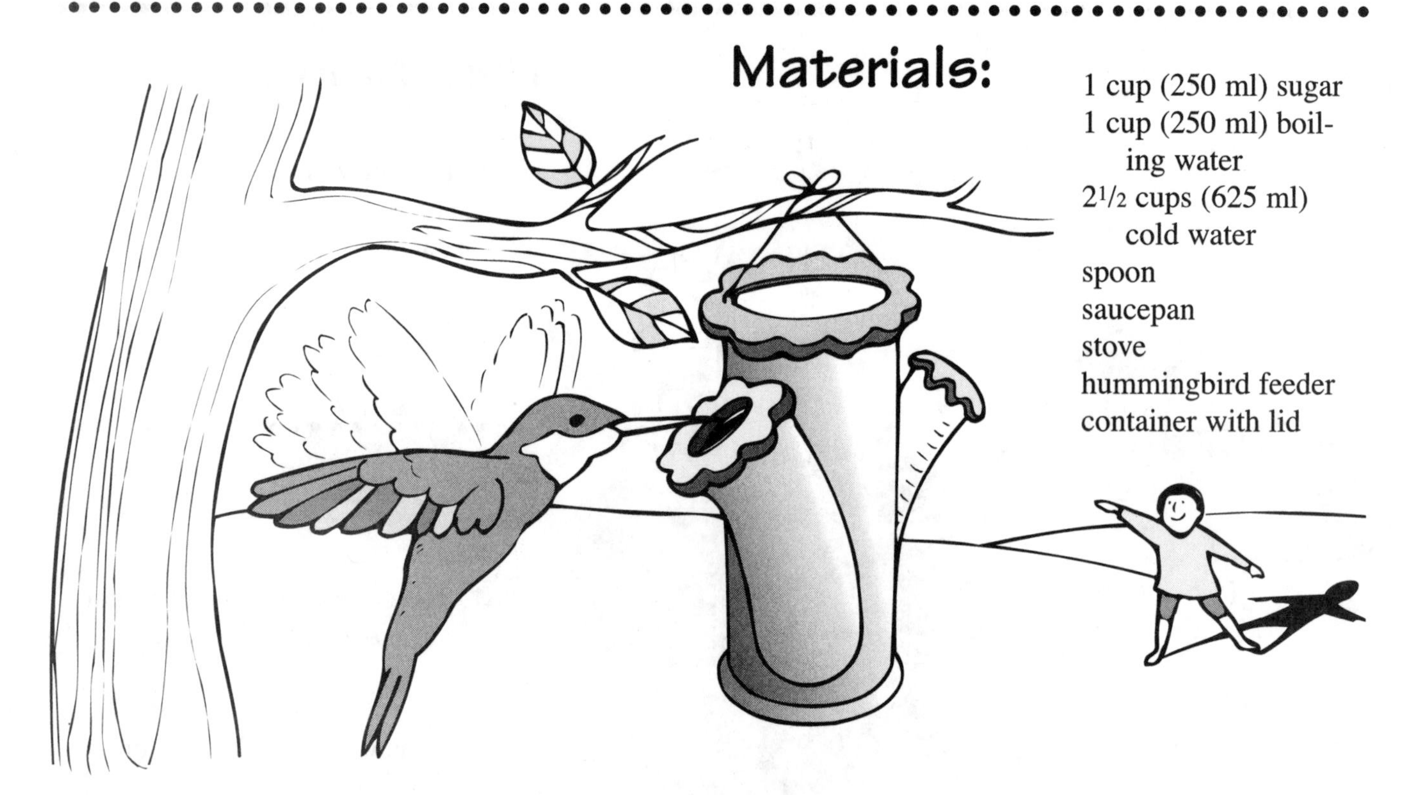

1 cup (250 ml) sugar
1 cup (250 ml) boiling water
$2\frac{1}{2}$ cups (625 ml) cold water
spoon
saucepan
stove
hummingbird feeder
container with lid

Process:

1. Boil water in saucepan.
2. Add sugar to the boiling water and stir until the mixture is clear.
3. Add $2\frac{1}{2}$ cups (625 ml) of cold water.
4. Pour into bird feeder and refrigerate remaining food in the container with lid.

Try This:

- Hang the feeder outside your classroom window.
- Provide research materials so students can find out all sorts of interesting trivia about this little bird. They will be interested to know that the hummingbird's nest would fit in their palm. They eat flower nectar, small insects and spiders. They are very aggressive. They will *even* fight bumblebees. They can fly, hover in mid-air, speed forward and stop with amazing accuracy and speed.

* Caution: Be careful with hot liquid!

Rover's Snack

K-3   

For the dog in your life.

Materials:

water
1/4 cup (60 ml) beef broth
1 package active dry yeast
1 tsp (5 ml) sugar
1 1/2 cups (375 ml) tomato juice
1 cup (250 ml) all-purpose flour
1 1/2 cups (375 ml) wheat germ
2 1/2 cups (625 ml) whole wheat flour
large bowl
spoon
cutting board
knife
rolling pin
spatula
cookie sheet
stove

Process:

1. Preheat oven to 300°F (154°C).
2. Stir water and broth in bowl.
3. Add yeast and let stand for 5 minutes.
4. Add tomato juice, 1 cup (250 ml) all-purpose flour and wheat germ.
5. Stir with a large spoon until mixture forms a batter.
6. Add the remaining all-purpose and whole wheat flours.
7. Dig in and stir with your hands.
8. Form dough into small balls and place on floured cutting board.
9. Roll the balls with the rolling pin to about 1/4" (.6 cm) thick.
10. Use a sharp knife to cut the flattened dough into dog bone shapes.
11. Use a spatula to put your bones on a cookie sheet.
12. Bake at 300°F (154°C) for one hour, turn oven off and leave bones in oven for 4 hours.

Try This:

- Make this a "gift" for Christmas or a special day devoted to animals–for your pet, a grandparent's or a friend's.
- Integrate with a unit on pets.
- Write the recipe on chart paper. Assign each task to a student or group of students.
- Incorporate math measuring and time lessons with this recipe. Assign students to measure and time the activity.

Squirrel Cobs

1-3  

A simple treat to make for the furry critters.

Materials:

string
cobs of corn (1 per child)

Process:

1. Husk the corn, leaving a 1" (2.54 cm) piece of stalk at the end of the cob.
2. Tie string firmly around the end of the stalk so the corn will hang. This may take several knots and rounds of string.
3. Hang the corn from a tree or other overhanging area where the squirrels can feast and you can watch!

Try This:

- Incorporate this activity with a study of squirrels or corn.
- Discuss various locations for hanging the cob of corn. Why might some locations be more desirable than others?
- Hang the cobs out for the squirrels for a special holiday–Thanksgiving or Christmas perhaps.
- Plant the corn with your class in the spring and "harvest" it with your new class in the fall. (You might like to share it with your previous student's classes.)
- Smooth the earth beneath the hanging cob and go back later to study squirrel tracks.
- Do not use plastic or wire in place of the string (even if the squirrels bite through the string and run off with the corn!)—it would be harmful to other animals.

Catch a Scent

Petrified Orange

1-3   

Materials:

For each student:
1/2 cup (125 ml) cloves
small thin-skinned orange
paper bag
ribbon

Process:

1. Stick cloves in orange in an interesting pattern that covers almost the entire surface of the orange.

2. Place in a paper bag in a cool place until the fruit has dried out–about three weeks.

3. Remove, add a bright ribbon and hang your petrified orange pomander. The spicy smell will last for years.

Try This:

- Make this for a gift for a special day like Mother's Day, Grandparents' Day or Christmas.
- Set up a Center for the Senses where students can smell various spices and substances. Use blindfolds and play a guessing game with strong scented items.

Potpourri Satchels

K-3  

Materials:

herbs or spices (cinnamon, ginger, cloves or anise)
dried flowers (find flowers with a scent)
8" (20.32 cm) square pieces of cheesecloth, netting or muslin
ribbon or string
grinding stone
scissors

Process:

1. Separate flower petals.
2. Crush herbs or spices with fingers or on a grinding stone.
3. Place flowers and spices into the center of the material.
4. Tie securely with ribbon or string.
5. Use a satchel to scent your drawer or give as a gift.

Try This:

- Take students on a hike to search for materials for this activity. You might make use of a plant and wildflower identification guide.
- Dry your own herbs, spices or flowers by hanging them upside down in a dry place.

Homemade Perfume

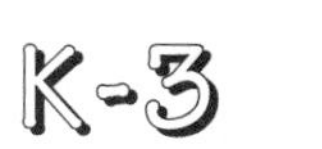

Materials:

grinding stone
selection of lemons, limes, apples, herbs, mint leaves, rose petals, lavender leaves
water
sieve
small glass containers with tight-fitting lids
bottle

Process:

1. Break the scent material with your fingers and then on grinding stone.
2. Place this material into the bottle.
3. Fill to the top with water.
4. Let sit in the sunshine for one day. If the liquid does not smell like the plants and flowers, add more material and let sit a little longer.
5. Pour clear liquid through sieve into fancy containers.
6. Seal the bottle with a cap or cork. Use within a few days.

Try This:

- Decorate a baby food jar or fancy bottle and give perfume as a gift to someone special.
- Experiment with mixing foods, herbs and flowers to invent your own unique scents.

* Caution: Ensure that sutdents are using the suggested flowers and plants, or non-poisonous alternatives.

Soapy Sculptures

K-3

10-60 min.

Materials:

2 cups (480 ml) Ivory Snow™ detergent
4 T (60 ml) water
food coloring
bowl

Process:

1. Pour detergent in bowl.
2. Mix water and food coloring to desired shade.
3. Using your hands, gradually work colored water into soap until it forms a clay of sorts.
4. Add more water if the mixture is too dry or more soap if it is too wet to work.
5. Sculpt into interesting shapes.
6. This soap can be used at school on messy little hands or given on special days as a welcome, practical gift.

Try This:

- Young children can shape snowballs and snowmen with this soap.
- Let students experiment with colors.
- Make soap eggs and put them in an egg carton.
- Incorporate this activity with a unit on pioneers and their soap-making techniques.

Chapter 7

Creations to Burn

A neat way to use old crayon stubs and create something wonderful to light up the dark!

- Candles are easy to make but call for safety precautions. These wax wonders are too good to pass up–so invite volunteers, stress the importance of caution around wax and proceed. Use your judgement and allow students to participate only where you feel it is appropriate for your particular group.

Homemade Candles

2-3 

Materials:

cans or sturdy cardboard containers such as milk cartons
crayon or candle stubs, paraffin or beeswax (1 lb [.45 kg] for four 2" [5.08 cm] candles)
large tin can
saucepan
candle wicking (available at craft supply stores)
small stick (craft stick or pencil)
tape
stove

Process:

1. Peel wrappers from used crayons and break into small pieces. Drop into old pan or coffee can, set in a pan of warm water on the stove.
2. Heat at medium heat until the wax is melted.
3. Pour the warm wax into the container.
4. Tape one end of the wick to a stick, hang the wick in the center of the candle resting the stick on the sides of the container.
5. Let the candle harden for 8 hours.
6. Peel away the conatiner.
7. Trim the wick.

Try This:

- For striped candles, let layers of different colors harden before pouring in the next layer.
- Wicks can be predipped in a hard wax available from dental office suppliers, or wicks can be hung over can with a weighted end to keep the wick taut.
- Pour wax into blown out eggs through one open end.

* Caution: Be extremely careful when heating and handling wax!

Sand Candles

1-3 

Materials:

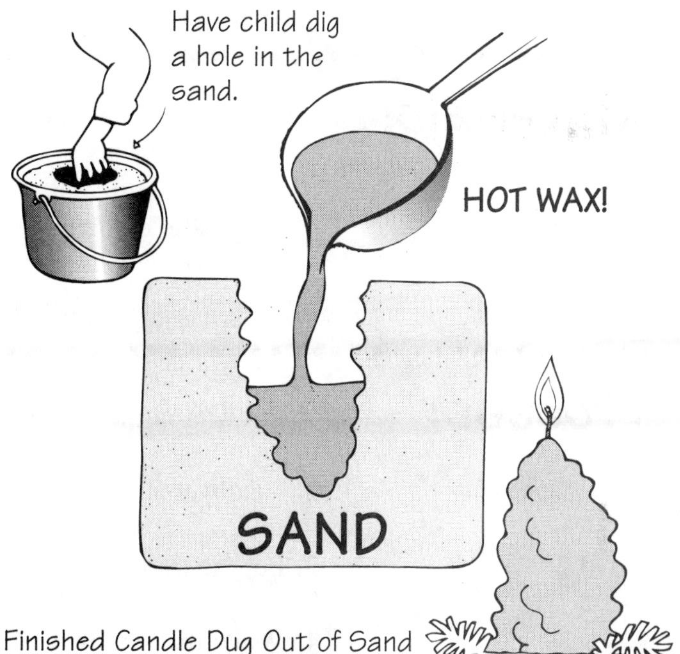

large basin full of sand, sand table or sand pit
crayons, candle stubs, beeswax or paraffin wax (1 lb [.45 kg] makes three or four 2" [5.08 cm] candles)
tin
double boiler
water
pot holders
small stone
small stick (craft stick or pencil)
candle wicking (available at craft supply stores)
trowel

Process:

1. Dig a hole in the sand about 4" (10.16 cm) wide and 8" (20.32 cm) deep.
2. Peel papers off crayon stubs. Break crayons into small bits and put in a tin.
3. Attach one end of the wick to the stick and the other to a stone.
4. Fill the pot halfway with hot water.
5. Put the tin of wax in the water and warm at low heat until the wax has melted. As the wax melts you can add more pieces and stir.
6. Carefully carry the tin of wax to the hole in the sand and pour in the wax.
7. Lower the wick into the middle of the wax. The stone will weigh it down, and the stick will hold the wick straight.
8. Allow the wax to cool and harden completely. This will take about 6 hours.
9. Use a trowel to ease the sand away from the candle. Lift the candle out.
10. Brush off excess, trim the wick and admire.

* Caution: Be careful when heating and handling wax!

Try This:

- Children dig the sand holes and dig their candles out but observe the wax melting and pouring.
- Students can place interesting objects around the edges of the sand hole. These will become part of the candle when the wax hardens.

Snow Candles

1-3  

Materials:

crayon stubs, candle stubs or paraffin wax
container: milk carton, glass or plastic container
prewaxed candle wick
small stick (craft stick or pencil)
small stone
tape
pot
tin can

Process:

1. Put wax in the tin can.
2. Heat water in a pot.
3. Put the tin of wax in the pot and melt the wax.
4. When the wax is thoroughly melted, take the tin outside.
5. Dig a hole in the snow where wax will be poured.
6. Tie or tape one of the prewaxed wick ends to the stick. Attach the other end to the stone.
7. Pour the wax into the snow.
8. Hang the wick into the wax with the stone weighing the wick down and the stick resting across the top of the snow.
9. As the ice and snow melt, the edges will harden and your candle will take on a delicate design.
10. Let the candle harden thoroughly before moving–about 3 hours.

Try This:

- Have students dig the "snow mold" for the wax that will be poured by an adult.
- Variation: Bring snow into the classroom and pack around edges of containers. The wax will be poured into the individual snow-packed containers.

* Caution: Be careful when heating and handling wax!

Rubber Dessert Eggs

1-3 

Colorful eggs you can eat. Makes 6 large eggs.

Materials:

2 envelopes unflavored gelatin
1 package (3 ounces [88.71 kg]) fruit-flavored gelatin
$1\frac{1}{2}$ cups (375 ml) boiling water
prepared eggshells
large needle
bowls
measuring cup
funnel

Process:

1. Wash eggs and with a large needle, pierce the narrow end of the egg breaking the membrane and yolk. Make a hole about $\frac{1}{2}$" (1.25 cm) wide.
2. Hold egg over small bowl and shake the contents out.
3. Rinse the inside of the egg well and let dry thoroughly (narrow end up) in egg carton.
4. In a medium bowl, combine unflavored gelatin and flavored gelatin.
5. Add boiling water and stir until gelatin is completely dissolved.
6. Cool 10 minutes.
7. Using a measuring cup and funnel, pour mixture into hole in eggshells.
8. Chill until firm–about 2 hours.
9. Peel the outer shell of the egg and then the membrane to reveal the shimmery, jewel-like egg you can eat. The eggs will stay firm, smooth and shiny at room temperature.

Try This:

- Serve at Easter or for a spring unit.
- Incorporate this activity with a study of eggs.
- Make a nest of lettuce leaves to serve these.
- Discuss how the eggs feel and look.
- Play a game of Pass the Egg–every student has a spoon, and the eggs are passed from spoon to spoon. Make it a cooperative effort that builds group and fine motor skills.

Apple Leather

A fun, healthy chew!

Materials:

6 firm apples
apple peeler
knife
string
darning needle
paper bag

Process:

1. Peel the apples.
2. Cut out the cores.
3. Slice apples into pieces about 1/2" (1.25 cm) thick.
4. Put about a yard of string through the eye of a darning needle.
5. Thread the apple pieces onto the string like beads. Don't let the apple pieces touch one another. Use extra strings if you need them.
6. Hang up the strings like a food clothesline.
7. Turn the apples every other day.
8. Remove the leather apple rings on the seventh day, and eat them or store them in a paper bag for later.

Try This:

- Integrate this activity with a study of harvest.
- Talk about nutrition.
- Observe the changes on a daily basis.

Melon Bowl

1-3

Materials:

1 large watermelon
1 cantaloupe melon
1 other seasonal melon
berries in season
blunt knives
sharp knife
melon baller
fruit cups
spoons
cutting board

Process:

1. Cut the melon in half.
2. Have children remove the insides of the melon with spoons until only the shell remains. Reserve the insides on the cutting board.
3. Allow children to cut the melon into bite-size pieces using blunt knives. (Melon is very easy to cut!)
4. Children can use the melon baller to get scoops of watermelon, cantaloupe, etc.
5. Put all of the melon pieces into the melon bowl.
6. Add seasonal fruit, toss and serve.

Try This:

- Grow your own melons with the children if the seasons permit in your area.
- Invite children to design their own way of making melon shapes. Do cookie cutters work? What happens when different kinds of spoons are used?
- Save the melon seeds for seed pictures, jewelry or manipulative math activities. (Be prepared for seed spitting contests–use your own discretion!)
- Use this as an end-of-the-year treat.

* Caution: Use very blunt knives!

Yogurt Pops

K-3  

Materials:

To make approximately 20 pops:
2 cups (500 ml) plain yogurt
1 1/4 cups (310 ml) frozen concentrated orange juice
1 tsp (5 ml) vanilla
bowl
spoon
ice cube trays
craft sticks

Process:

1. Place the yogurt, frozen juice and vanilla in the bowl.
2. Stir hard until everything is mixed together.
3. Scrape the mixture into ice cube trays.
4. Place a wooden craft stick in each cube.
5. Put the trays into the freezer and leave at least 4 hours.

Try This:

- For different flavors, use frozen grape or pineapple juice instead of orange juice.
- Talk about nutritious treats. Make a chart. Help students to recognize what is good for their bodies.

Ice Berries

Materials:

berries (in season)
cookie sheet
colander
drying cloth
freezer

Process:

1. Pick or purchase fresh berries.
2. Wash berries in a colander.
3. Allow berries to drain and dry thoroughly. Gentle drying with a towel will speed this process along.
4. On a cookie sheet, space the berries so they are not touching, and place them in the freezer until frozen, about 30 to 60 minutes depending upon the berry size.
5. Remove berries from freezer and add to drinks to chill as you would with ice cubes.

Try This:

- Freeze smaller berries in clumps. Try shaping these into creatures.
- Drop small berries in ice cube trays, add water and freeze. The fruit will appear to "float" inside of the ice cube.
- Incorporate this activity into a study of changes in the state of matter, temperature or weather.
- Have students experiment with the length of time it takes different berries to freeze and thaw. Does size make a difference? Why or why not? Does a wrapped berry freeze and thaw at a different rate?
- Try freezing other fruits–lemons, oranges, cherries, peaches and melon. How do they change? Discuss methods of preserving foods used in the past and the present.

* Caution: Small berries can be a choking hazard!

Ice Arrangements

Materials:

container (small plastic margarine tub or cutoff milk carton)
water
assortment of berries, fruit, mint leaves or edible flower petals
freezer

Process:

1. Fill the container half full with water.
2. Freeze until hard.
3. Brush water on the ice and arrange flowers, fruit, berries or petals on the ice.
4. Freeze until arrangement stays in place–about 30 minutes.
5. Cover arrangement with water and freeze again.
6. Remove from freezer and let thaw until the ice arrangement can be popped from the container. This can be achieved more quickly if the container is set in hot water for 5 minutes.
7. Float the arrangment in a punch bowl or lemonade pitcher.

Try This:

- Have each child make an ice arrangement or "ice pie" and display outside on a cold day–or for a short time on a hot day.
- Freeze a wooden stick frame inside a square pan. Create a picture inside the frame using various visually interesting items. Cover with water and freeze again. Remove from the pan and admire the framed ice masterpiece. String can be looped and frozen in the back of the picture so that the artwork can be hung outside in the winter.

Green Things

K-3  

Sprout some seeds and eat 'em up.

Materials:

2 T (30 ml) of untreated seeds–alfalfa, mung (bean sprouts), soybeans, fenugreek, radishes, peas, sesame, wheat, corn–available at health food, organic or Asian food stores. Most garden seeds are chemically treated–use only those that state otherwise.
cold water
sprouting container (margarine tub, ice-cream container, etc.)
mesh netting
elastic band

Process:

1. Put the seeds in the sprouting container and cover with cold water.
2. Cover with the mesh netting. Hold in place with the elastic band.
3. Soak overnight.
4. In the morning turn the sprouting container upside down over a bowl to drain the seeds.
5. Rinse the sprouts with fresh water two to three times each day. Keep them drained but moist.
6. When the seeds sprout tails–usually between two and five days–they are ready to be eaten. When they taste best to you, put them in the refrigerator to stop their growth.

Try This:

- Eat the sprouts raw or cooked. Make sandwiches, salads, stir fry or a soup for a class lunch or snack.
- Have the children experiment and record. Do the beans sprout faster in warmth or cold?
- What differences are noted when the sprouts are kept in the sun versus darkness?
- Students can role-play at being sprouts. What happens when "sun" shines down or "rain" falls on the seeds?
- This activity will integrate well into a study of plants or growth.

Sesame Snacks

1-3 

Good-for-you candy. Sweet and nutritious!

Materials:

- 1/2 cup (125 ml) peanut butter
- 1/2 cup (125 ml) liquid honey
- 1 cup (250 ml) skim milk powder
- 1 cup (250 ml) sesame seeds
- 2 T (30 ml) chopped nuts
- 1/2 cup (125 ml) shredded coconut
- saucepan
- spoon
- cake pan
- stove

Process:

1. Measure peanut butter and honey into the saucepan.
2. Place over medium heat.
3. Cook and stir for 3 minutes.
4. Remove the saucepan from the heat.
5. Add the skim milk powder, sesame seeds, coconut and nuts.
6. Stir until everything is well mixed.
7. Press the mixture into the cake pan.
8. Place the pan in the refrigerator until the mixture becomes firm–about 2 hours.
9. Cut into squares.

Try This:

- Enhance a study of seeds with this tasty treat.
- Allow students to taste ingredients individually and then in the end product. Can they distinguish any single taste in the finished recipe?

* Caution: Be careful when using heat source!

Candied Flowers

K-3  

Materials:

- 2 egg whites
- 1/2 cup (125 ml) flower petals
- 1/2 cup (125 ml) sugar
- whisk
- wire rack
- pastry or clean paintbrush

Process:

1. Gather petals of chemical-free roses or violets–confirm with an identification guide before eating.
2. Gently wash the petals and spread on a wire rack to dry.
3. Whisk the egg whites until frothy.
4. Carefully paint the petals with the egg whites.
5. Sprinkle sugar over the petals and let dry thoroughly until hard.
6. Eat as they are or use to decorate cupcakes or ice cream.

Try This:

- Introduce students to the idea that weeds and wildflowers are valuable sources of food and medicines.
- Use a field guide to help you identify the plants you eat.

* Caution: Remind children that nothing from the wild should be eaten without an adult's verification of its identity!

Curds and Whey

K-3  

Great for eating during a nursery rhyme theme.

Materials:

1 cup (250 ml) fresh milk
2 T (30 ml) white vinegar
spoon
jar

Process:

1. Fill the jar with milk and vinegar.

2. Stir.

3. Let stand for 3 minutes.

4. The milk will separate into the white solid curds and clear liquid whey.

5. Enjoy the curds right away or store in a cool place.

Try This:

- Use this activity to enhance a study of nursery rhymes, the dairy farm, pioneers or nutrition.

Butter

K-3  

Betty Botter never bought it so good!

Materials:

$^{1}/_{2}$ pint (.235 l) heavy cream (whipping cream)
marble
jar with secure lid
salt (optional)
container

Process:

1. Pour cream into jar.
2. Add marble.
3. Put lid on tightly.
4. Shake, shake, shake your way to butter!
5. Pour the buttermilk off and remove the marble.
6. Add a little salt if desired, and put the butter in a container.
7. Eat right away or store in a cool place for later.

Try This:

- Extend a lesson about pioneers with this activity.
- Set up a Tasting Center where students taste various butters and margarines.
- Allow children to experiment with their butter by adding more or less salt, yellow food coloring and a bit of sugar.
- A bread-making activity would go well with this project!
- Ask students to recall and write about the activity.

Peanut Butter

K-3    

Materials:

peanuts roasted in shells
1 T (15 ml) corn oil
blender
bowl or jar
friends

Process:

1. Gather friends to help shell the peanuts.
2. Shell enough peanuts to make 1 cup (250 ml).
3. Rub the red skins off the peanuts.
4. Place the oil in the blender and put on the lid.
5. Turn the blender on.
6. Drop the peanuts a few at a time through the hole in the lid of the blender.
7. Stop blending when the peanut butter is as smooth as you like it.
8. Scrape the peanut butter into a bowl or jar.
9. Eat it right away or store it in a sealed container.

Try This:

- Allow children to taste and compare various butters–apple, peanut, dairy.
- What animals eat peanuts? Do they like peanut butter?
- Read and write stories and poems about peanut butter.

Ice Cream

K-3  

Materials:

1 pint (.47 l) thick cream
1/3 cup (80 ml) sugar or honey
1 tsp (5 ml) vanilla
1 pinch of table salt
aluminum can with a plastic lid
large pot, bowl or pail
wooden spoon with a hole in it
crushed ice cubes, icicles or snow
box of table salt (or rock salt from the hardware store)

Process:

1. Pour the thick cream into the aluminum can.
2. Add sugar, a pinch of salt and the vanilla and stir well.
3. Poke a hole large enough for the spoon handle in the plastic lid of the aluminum can.
4. Push the spoon handle through the hole and fit the lid onto the can.
5. Fill the base of the pot, bowl or pail with ice. Set the can of the cream mixture on top of the ice.
6. Pour a layer of salt on the ice. Continue layering the ice and salt around the tin until it reaches the top of the tin.
7. Let stand for 5 minutes.
8. Have children take turns twirling the spoon handle to mix the ice cream. Turn the can occasionally.
9. Continue adding layers of ice and salt as the ice melts.
10. After about 15 minutes the spoon will become quite difficult to twirl–this means the ice cream is freezing! Continue twirling until the ice cream has the consistency you desire.
11. When the ice cream has the consistency you desire, remove the can from the ice bucket, remove the spoon from the lid and serve! (If you desire a firmer ice cream, the mixture can be covered and placed in the freezer for about 1 hour.

Try This:

- Experiment with a variety of flavors–berries, fruits, extracts, coffee, chocolate, etc. Stir these in when you are ready to stop twirling or just before you put the mixture in the freezer.
- Read and write stories about ice cream.
- Hand out play money and set up an ice-cream store as part of your math lesson.
- Introduce the concepts of melting and freezing.
- For some added fun, try to eat the ice cream with chopsticks.
- Invent a new ice-cream cone. What else would do the trick?

Concoctions Bibliography

Atwood, Margaret. Illustrated by John Bianchi. *For the Birds*. Douglas & McIntyre, Toronto, 1990.

Bakule, Paula Dreifus, Ed., *Rodale's Book of Practical Formulas: Easy-to-Make, Easy-to-Use Recipes for Hundreds of Everyday Activities and Tasks*. U.S. Rodale Press, Inc., 1991.

Bell, J.L. Illustrated by Bill Kimber. *Soap Science: A Science Book Bubbling with 36 Experiments*. Kids Can Press, Toronto, 1993. U.S. Distribution: Addison-Wesley.

Better Homes and Gardens. Water Wonders. Meredith Corporation, Des Moines, Iowa. 1989.

Canadian Wildlife Federation/Western Regional Environmental Education Council & the Western Regional Environmental Education Council & the Western Association of Fish and Wildlife Agencies. *Project Wild: Elementary Activity Guide*. Canadian Wildlife Federation, Ottawa, Canada, 1988.

Diehn, Gwen, and Terry Kratwurst. *Nature Crafts for Kids: 50 Fantastic Things to Make with Mother Nature's Help*. Sterling Publishing Co., Inc., New York, 1992.

Erickson, Donna. Illustrated by David LaRochelle. *Prime Time Together . . . with Kids*. Discovery Toys, Augsburg Fortress, Minneapolis, 1989.

Gold, Carol. *The Jumbo Book of Science: 136 of the Best Experiments from the Ontario Science Center.* Kids Can Press, Toronto, 1994. U.S. Distribution: Addison-Wesley.

Graham, Ada. *Foxtails, Ferns and Fish Scales: A Handbook of Art and Nature Projects*. Four Winds Press, 1976.

Gray, Magda. *Rainy Day Pastimes: 215 Ideas to Keep Kids Happy*. Marshall Cavendish, London, 1975.

Griffin, Margaret, and Ruth Griffin. *It's a Gas!* Kids Can Press, Toronto, 1993. U.S. Distribution: IPG Distribution.

Klutz Press Editors. *Everybody's Everywhere Backyard Bird Book.* Klutz Press, Palo Alto, CA, 1992.

Norris, Doreen, and Joyce Boucher. *Observing Children in the Formative Years*. The Board of Education for the city of Toronto, Toronto, 1980.

Wilkes, Angela. *My First Cook Book*. Stoddart Publishing, Toronto, 1989.

Creations

Foreword

Kid Creations is a lively collection of recipes for art supplies and creative suggestions for implementing these in the primary classroom. This section is designed to generate fun, skill-based experiences in the primary art program. Children will have the opportunity to explore, express themselves freely and experience the pure joy of creating.

Acknowledgements

I would like to thank the many children who have made this section possible through their yearning to explore and create–especially Kiersten, Ben and Bailey who can make anything out of anything. Thanks to Charlie for his ideas, to Al and Sandy Cochrane (my parents) for their artistic influence, to Tracey Coveart for her editing and to Carol Goulette for sharing her creativity.

I am grateful to all of the inventive individuals who directly or inadvertently have contributed to this compilation for the past 16 years. Your recipes are continuing to excite children!

I would also like to thank all of the creative educators, parents, outdoor recreation leaders and summer camp staffs for their experimentation, keen interest and ability to pass their enthusiasm on to children.

Table of Contents

Skill Development

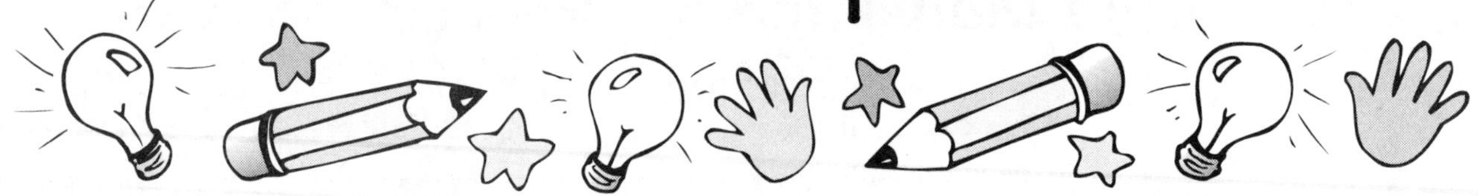

Art media offers rich opportunity for the development of many skills. The materials and activities suggested in this section can be used as needed to facilitate the development of various skills. Refer to these words to see which skills are targeted by a particular activity.

Intellectual

Social

Emotional

Physical Development (fine and gross motor)

Language

Curriculum Links

Each of the activities can be extended and incorporated into the study of a wider topic, and cross into various curriculum areas. Within the areas listed below, the materials and projects can be used to help develop any number of concepts. These words are used to indicate which curriculum area an activity most easily fits into.

Language

Math

Art

Science

Geography

History

Physical Education

Health

Music

Guidelines to Facilitate Creative Learning

1. Respect a child's right to create.
   Allow children to explore with materials and express their *own* ideas.
   Introduce skills, techniques and tools in response to a child's curiosity and needs.
   Once students have had the opportunity for free exploration of materials, then tools, props, suggestions, models and samples can be provided to further develop and introduce particular skills.

2. Organize in advance. Read instructions, have materials ready to go and make a sample in a trial run of the activity. Kids should be able to explore and create with little or no educator assistance.

3. Provide ample creative space and materials for natural artistic exploration.

4. Have flexible expectations and expect unpredictable results.

5. Show appreciation of children's exploration by recognizing their efforts as artistic accomplishments. Show interest, give positive comments and let the child volunteer information.

6. Evaluate the child's growth through observation of a wide variety of artistic experiences. Focus on the process of creating, not the end product.

7. Expect things to get messy! Allow for creative problem solving and choices when you incorporate cleanup into the activity.

8. Provide a means to show or keep works as students will emotionally bond to these creations.

Chapter 1

Things to Create On

The Clean Slate

Surfaces to explore scribbles, lines and shapes are very important. Each child has unique responses to different surfaces. A sense of ownership comes with a self-made means and surfaces for creating and work on these becomes more meaningful.

Aims:

- To involve the child in the making of practical work surfaces.
- To encourage problem solving through the construction of various practical work surfaces.
- To encourage the development of group skills.
- To promote self-esteem in the child.

Objectives:

- Child will make various surfaces for later artistic activities.
- Child will develop fine and large motor skills through the making of these items.
- Child will experience a sense of self-work through making of these surfaces.

Skill Development:

- Intellectual
- Emotional
- Gross Motor
- Social
- Fine Motor
- Language

Curriculum Links:

- Language
- Science
- History
- Math
- Art

Homemade Felt Board

2-3  

This item can be used over and over again for various projects and activities.

Materials:

heavy cardboard or light wood panel board
felt piece, larger than the board
small felt bits in bright and contrasting colors
scissors
electric tape

Process:

1. Cover the board with felt. Wrap the felt around so that it is smooth on the front surface. Helping hands can keep the felt taut as it is pulled around to the back of the board.
2. Tape the felt on the back side of the board.
3. Cut various sized shapes, letters, characters and numbers from felt pieces.

Try This:

- Choose a theme and go wild with felt. Kids can create their own theme-oriented pieces. Teachers and students can use the board to talk about themes and concepts.
- Kids and educators can create felt puzzles to be pieced together on the board.
- Teachers and students can use the board as a wonderful medium for storytelling.
- Adhere fun shapes to boards individually, in small groups or as one large group.
- Use the board as a daily calendar in conjunction with a math program.

Homemade Chalkboard

K-3

Materials:

chalkboard paint (spray paint or tin from hobby or hardware stores)
heavy cardboard or masonite board
paintbrush
edging tape (masking, cloth or electric)
old sock
chalk

Process:

1. In a well-ventilated area, brush or spray chalkboard paint on the board. Let it dry completely.
2. Trim the edges of the board with tape.
3. The child's very own chalkboard is ready to use! See chalk recipe on page 14. The old sock that lost its mate can be used to erase.

Try This:

- Make one large board or individual chalkboards for each child.
- Challenge students to measure and tape their boards as neatly as possible.
- Children can individualize their boards with acrylic paint borders or logos.
- Incorporate measurement concepts in this activity.
- Provide colored chalk, tracers and alphabet cards.
- Use the boards for math lessons, to record bird-watching results, to keep tallies and to make pictures.
- Explore chalking techniques. Chalk on a damp board, use pointy chalk, the edge and the side of the chalk. How many different lines can you make?

* Caution: Paint in open air!

Recycled Paper

1-3 over 1 hour SPACE

Materials:

newspapers
bucket
water
wire whisk
3 T (15 ml) cornstarch
1 cup (250 ml) water
measuring spoons
piece of screen or wire mesh about 6" (15.24 cm) across
plastic wrap to cover screen

Process:

1. Tear newspapers into very small pieces and drop them in a bucket. (Students like to do this!)
2. When the bucket is half-full of newspaper pieces, add enough water to wet all of the pieces.
3. Let the soggy mess stand for at least two hours.
4. Using the whisk, beat the mess to a creamy pulp.
5. Dissolve cornstarch in 1 cup (250 ml) of water and mix in with the pulp.
6. Spread sheets of newspaper on a work surface large enough to lay the screen on.
7. Submerge the piece of screen into the mixture and gently lift it out. Repeat this several times until the screen has about 1/8" (.3 cm) of pulp on it.
8. Lay the pulp-covered screen on top of the newspaper-covered surface.
9. Cover the pulpy screen with plastic wrap.
10. Remove excess water from the screen by blotting over plastic with a towel. Children can take turns with this task.
11. Set the screen up so air can dry the pulp.
12. When dry, gently peel your recycled paper from screen.

Recycled Paper

1-3 over 1 hour SPACE

Try This:

- Use your recycled paper as a decorative paper for a special project.
- Make paper kites that fly with string or a simple kite that flies from a thin stick.
- Experiment with a large window screen to make a large piece of paper.
- Mix a batch of paper in the blender reducing recipe to fit the appliance.
- Pour the mixture into a clay mold. Remove when dry to create a raised form that can be painted and/or framed.
- Incorporate counting as students drop newspaper pieces into the bucket, one at a time, two at a time and so on. Estimate how many pieces it will take to half fill the bucket.
- Explore $^{1}/_{2}$" (1.25 cm), $^{1}/_{8}$" (.3 cm) and 1" (2.54 cm). What else in your room is $^{1}/_{8}$" (.3 cm) thick?
- How does the pulp turn into paper? Introduce the concept of evaporation.
- How long is two hours? While you wait for the messy mixture to be ready for stirring, turn paper making into a lesson on telling time.

Anything Paper

1-3

Materials:

lint (from clothes dryer)
cake pan
rags
choice of flowers, grass, weeds, leaves, paper towels, colored paper, newspaper
water
wire mesh or old screen (to fit pan)
heavy scissors

Process:

1. Cut wire mesh or old screen into a circle that fits easily inside a cake pan.
2. Place lint and gathered materials into cake pan.
3. Fill the pan with warm water to soak contents of pan and let stand for 5 minutes.
4. Prepare a rag-covered surface.
5. Submerge the screen into the mixture and lift out so that a layer of linty mush remains on top of the screen. Submerge again if you see any holes.
6. Blot the pulp very carefully with the rags.
7. Place the screen on a rag-covered surface to dry.
8. When the pulp is dry, gently remove it from the screen and admire your creation!

Try This:

- To the lint mixture, add very tiny bits of colored thread, dried grass, flowers, fabric pieces, weeds, etc. Encourage every student to contribute something. Admire and discuss the colors.
- Place lace, pressed flowers or leaves on the wet paper. These will dry into the paper.
- Add berries or other dye sources (see page 13) to the mixture for hued papers.
- Glue dried paper to used paper or construction paper and mat or frame.
- Ask children how the lint turned into paper. Introduce the concept of evaporation.
- Incorporate a lesson on time; have children time the five-minute waiting period.
- Challenge children to think about different kinds of paper. Children can suggest their own paper recipes.
- Incorporate a history lesson on the origins of paper. What did early people use?

Grinding Stone

K-3  

A treasured tool that becomes an important work surface. The more it is used, the better it gets.

Materials:

large flat stone
hard stone able to fit in hand easily

Process:

1. Grind objects between the large and small stones. In time, a depression will form that will make the grinding of various ingredients much easier.
2. Use this tool as needed to create ingredients needed for various recipes.

Try This:

- Try grinding grains.
- Discuss early methods of making paints, foods and medicines. Compare these to current methods.

Chapter 2

Things to Paint and Draw With

Vibrant colors, neat textures and lines of all sorts make works of art. A class can make what they need to form lines by raiding the kitchen cupboard, refrigerator, school shelves and school yard. Students will scribble, shade and make lines and shapes with homemade chalk, crayons that are hard to resist and paint kids can't wait to get a brush into!

The predictable stages of drawing; Experimentation and Scribble, Pre-Schematic, Schematic and Representational Stages will progress naturally as children are presented with intriguing opportunities to make lines with all sorts of tools. Whether a child attempts to produce a representation of an object or merely enjoys the process, painting and drawing will encourage thoughtful observation, develop fine motor skills and reinforce a positive self-concept.

Aims:

- To involve the child in varied drawing, coloring and painting activities.
- To encourage children to explore drawing, coloring and painting techniques.
- To investigate art media in a wide variety of conditions.

Objectives:

- Child will explore properties of various media.
- Child will explore and experiment with a variety of painting and drawing.
- Child will develop graduated skills through use of various media.
- Child will develop skill in the handling and care of particular tools.

Skill Development:

- Intellectual
- Emotional
- Large Motor
- Social
- Fine Motor
- Language

Curriculum Links:

- Language
- Science
- Geography
- Physical Education
- Math
- Art
- History
- Music

Natural Pigment

K-3  

Make the powdered colors needed to give your paints colors.

Materials:

grinding stone
smooth unbreakable surface (cutting board, Plexiglas™ , paper plate)
natural pigment sources: berries, mud, clay, dirt, soft stones, sand, plants
synthetic pigment sources: drink crystals, colored chalks

Process:

1. Search for and gather the things you need to make interesting colors.
2. Put the pigment source on the surface and grind with your rock.

Try This:

- Natural pigments, tempera, watercolor paints, water crayons or food coloring can be used to color paints.
- Set up a Color Center where children can make pigment, add it to various media and create.

Homemade Chalk

K-3 

Chalk is an excellent medium to create various textures, effects, colors and shades on all kinds of surfaces. Easy to make, stores well and cleans up in a flash.

Materials:

- 1 part water
- 2 parts plaster of Paris
- small paper roll, rubber bands and wrap or paper cups
- powdered tempera paint
- spoon
- mixing container
- cloth or face mask

Process:

1. If using paper rolls, cover bottom of roll with wrap and hold in place with rubber band.
2. Mix tempera in water until darker than desired shade is reached.
3. Pour colored water into mixing container.
4. Gently pour plaster on top of water, and let sit until the plaster settles to the bottom.
5. Stir mixture with spoon or hands until it forms a creamy mixture.
6. Pour into small paper cups or paper roll forms.
7. Let the mixture dry until hard–at least one hour.
8. Peel off the paper form (If the chalk is damp, you may need to rub the chalk to remove paper residue.) and start chalkin'!

Try This:

- Decorate the school yard–it will wash away with the rain!
- Teach a unit on the old favorite chalk games of the school yard.
- Incorporate a study of historical children's games around the world.
- Incorporate a lesson in time as you wait one hour for the mixture to harden.
- Experiment with color.
- Make texture rubbings using chalk.
- Have students trace one another's silhouettes onto the school yard.
- Make a picture using chalk. Paint over it with water for a marbled effect.
- Variation: Use ground eggshells in place of plaster of Paris. Grind eggshells with a grinding stone until fine. This chalk will work best on the sidewalk.
- Ask students to think about who uses chalk and why? Consider teachers, sign writers, ballerinas, gymnasts, tailors and dressmakers and many more.
- Ask students to think about uses of chalk. Did they know it is found in various artistic mediums, cement, toothpaste, makeup and fertilizer? Real chalk consists of the remains of microscopic sea creatures from the Cretaceous period. In ancient Rome chalk was called "creta."

* Caution: Do not ingest plaster dust; keep dust down!

Charcoal

2-3    

Materials:

charred wood
pocket knife or small saw
flat stone

Process:

1. All you have to do is find charred wood in the remains of a camp fire, fireplace or other place where wood has burned. You might find this opportunity on a field trip or nearby. You can even cheat and bring some charred wood to the classroom. Let kids break off chunks or cut pieces in a uniform manner with your pocket knife or small saw.
2. Rub the end of the charcoal stick on the stone to sharpen to a point.
3. Remember not to wear best whites for this activity and wash up after the picture making.

Try This:

- Charcoal works wonderfully on the homemade papers in this book or other thick papers.
- Use charcoal and thin paper to do rubbings of tree bark, brick walls and other interesting textures.
- Have students do five-minute charcoal sketches of "a model" in various poses.
- Talk about where charcoal comes from–part of a unit on trees perhaps.
- Study artwork completed by the masters in charcoal.
- Encourage kids to look around for subjects to sketch anytime, anyplace.

* Caution: Use caution when carving with pocket knife or saw.

Earth Colors

2-3

Materials:

2 ounces (56 g) beeswax
2 ounces (56 g) paraffin
5 tsp (25 ml) linseed oil
5 tsp (25 ml) natural pigment
old pan
spoon
old cupcake pan
foil cupcake cups
stove

Process:

1. Line the cupcake pan with foil cupcake cups.
2. Break up waxes and heat in pan over low heat until melted.
3. Remove from heat and slowly add oil and dry earth pigment to warm wax.
4. Stir until well mixed.
5. Pour warm mixture into cupcake cups and let cool.
6. Allow children to remove wax forms and have fun with earthy colors.

Try This:

- Allow students to choose earth pigments.
- Pour into paper rolls or other shapes to mold your crayons.
- Experiment with various waxes.
- Create a crayoned mural.
- An old paintbrush dipped in the almost-cool wax creates a neat effect on paper.
- Observe the progression in picture making from scribble to patches, to ovals, lines, dots, polliwogs and emerging head with significant features.
- Enhance a study of insects and bees.
- Embark on an investigation of crayons. How are they made? What colors are they?
- Talk about melting. What else melts? Observe ice cubes, gelatin and chocolate.

* Caution: Use extreme caution around heat and wax.

Egg Crayons

1-3     

Materials:

crayon stubs
empty eggshells
tin can
egg carton
stove

Process:

1. Adult helpers can make the egg blowing go much easier! Use a large pointy needle to break a large hole in the narrow end of an egg.
2. Shake the egg until all of the contents are out. Rinse the inside and leave the eggshell to dry in egg carton.
3. Peel wrappers from crayons and drop the stubs into the can.
4. Put the can in pan of hot water and melt stubs until squishy with a few chunks floating.
5. Pour chunky wax into eggshells in egg carton. Fill each egg to the top.
6. Let the wax cool and harden (place in freezer for quick hardening).
7. Peel away eggshell to find a wax egg that really colors.
8. Store coloring eggs in an egg carton.

Try This:

- Give as a gift (great in spring).
- Mix colors for a rainbow effect.
- If time and resources are limited, break eggshells in half and set in carton.
- Melt crayon stubs in muffin tins in oven on low for some rainbow muffin crayons.
- Try "Alpha-Doodles"–turn letters into doodley characters.
- Cover an entire page with crayon color. Next, cover it all with black crayon, and then scratch off the black using a point or edge for a startling effect.
- Embark on a study of crayons, colors or shapes.

* Caution: Hot wax!

Invisible Ink

K-3

What could be better for a quick and simple secret message?

Materials:

citrus juice
white paper
writing instruments (paintbrush, cotton swab, toothpick, feather, pen nib)
small bowl
heat source (toaster, light bulb, hot radiator) NEVER use an open flame!

Process:

1. Squeeze juice from an orange, lemon or grapefruit into a small container.
2. Write a secret message on white paper using a writing instrument and juice.
3. Heat the note to reveal the message. When the message receiver wants to read this mysterious message, he must heat it up over a toaster or close to a light bulb with assistance. Stop heating as soon as the message appears.

Try This:

- Incorporate with a study of detectives, Halloween or mystery.
- Encourage interest in the written word with these invisible messages.
- Set up a Writing Center. What creative substances can the students think of to write with? Offer the juice as a medium for messages. Discuss the results of this effort. Have students guess what will happen when the message is heated. Investigate why this happens.

* Caution: Be careful when using heat source.

Paints

Children can roll up their sleeves and dig their hands into some slippery, colorful fun with finger paints or grab a brush and create masterpieces. Exploration with paints appears to have the added benefit of soothing kids and adults. Provide the opportunity to paint whenever you feel it is needed. Most powdered paints will wash out, but food coloring will stain, so have paint smocks available.

Safe "Oil" Paint

K-3  

An earth friendly, kid safe, shiny alternative to oils. It responds like the paints of the masters.

Materials:

small containers
stir sticks
natural pigment
vegetable oil

Process:

1. Put a little pigment in each container.
2. Add oil to each container and stir.
3. Add enough oil to give the texture you want for your project.
4. Allow projects to dry overnight.

Try This:

- Children can create interesting textures by adding unusual ingredients to any paint recipe–provide salt, coffee grounds, whole wheat flour, sand, vanilla, cinnamon, perfume, liquid soap, talcum powder, glitter, grain and rice for a start!
- Cover dark paper with a thick layer of paint. While the paint is wet, make designs through the paint with various objects.
- This thick paint works well for hand paintings. Try a large mural.
- Try using sponges or rags to create interesting designs.
- Use this as a steppingstone for a study of art history.
- Discuss texture and the senses. Take students on a "texture hunt." Record their findings.
- Provide materials at a texture table where students can create substances of various textures.

Egg Tempera

K-3 10-60 min.

Materials:

2 eggs
mixing bowl
water
spoon
containers
natural pigment
vegetable oil

Process:

1. Crack two raw eggs into a bowl. Separate the eggs and save the yolks.
2. Add a little bit of water and stir until you make a smooth, runny syrup. Pour it into several small containers.
3. Add pigment to each dish to create the colors you want.
4. Paint with your egg tempera paint on heavy paper or cloth.

Try This:

- Use nature to make interesting prints. Find leaves or flowers, press into the painting and remove. It will leave a print of the plant.
- Cut fruit or vegetables in half and make prints. Press the cut side into the paint and gently press onto paper and lift off.

Mud Paint

K-3     

Materials:

mud
tray
sieve or sifter
bowl
blunt knife or craft stick
water
pigment
paper
paintbrushes
jars with lids

Process:

1. Gather the main ingredient–mud–from just about anywhere. (Use sterile potting soil if you are unsure about your outdoor sources.)
2. Strain the mud through a sieve or sifter.
3. Spread the strained mud on a tray to dry in the sun.
4. When dry, place in a bowl. Add a few drops of water and some pigment.
5. Mix with a craft stick or blunt knife until the mixture is paint-like. Add water to thin paint or dirt to thicken it. Kids will love to experiment.
6. Dip a paintbrush in and experiment with a new paint.
7. Store the dry paint indefinitely in jars with lids and labels.

Try This:

- Kids can finger paint with this stuff for a neat textural experience.
- Collection of the mud can be an adventure in itself.
- Tie this activity in with a geology study of rocks, the effect of wind and tides on rocks and a microscopic study of the grains of sand.
- Incorporate into a unit on science or geography.

Splatter Paint

K-3  

A great new way to paint beautiful masterpieces of bursting color! Introduces kids to motor skills involved in squirting and spraying. Provides new forms to be described and observed.

Materials:

4 cups (1000 ml) flour
1 cup (250 ml) salt
1/2 cup (125 ml) sugar
powdered tempera paint
5 cups (1250 ml) water
bristol board or heavy paper
spoon
bowl
funnel
squirt top or large-hole spray bottles (liquid soap containers, glue bottles, plant sprayers)

Process:

1. Measure and mix dry ingredients in a bowl.
2. Add water and stir until there are no lumps.
3. Use a funnel to pour this mixture into a squirt bottle.
4. Cover the work area with newspaper and squirt, spray and splatter away! Heavy papers (including the kind you make) and bristol board work best.
5. Lay creations flat to dry.

Try This:

- Tip and wiggle creations before the paint dries for fascinating dribble pictures.
- Frame these masterpieces with a plain border to set them off effectively.
- Put your wet painting in a tray or box lid with some marbles. Tip and tilt to get the marbles rolling for an amazing effect.

Glitter Squeeze Paint

K-3  

Materials:

1 cup (250 ml) flour
1 cup (250 ml) salt
1 cup (250 ml) water
food coloring
spoon
bowl
squeeze-top bottles
funnel
heavy paper or cardboard

Process:

1. Mix flour, salt and water together in bowl until well blended.
2. Add food coloring until you get the desired color.
3. Pour into squeeze bottles.
4. Squeeze onto heavy paper.
5. Let thoroughly dry for glittery effect.

Try This:

- Food coloring can stain. Students should wear painting smocks for this activity.
- Paint fireworks scenes on black construction paper.

Soapy Paint

K-3 10 min.

Materials:

$^1/_2$ cup (125 ml) hot tap water
soap flakes to desired thickness
eggbeater
food coloring
pan

Process:

1. Pour $^1/_2$ cup (125 ml) hot tap water in pan.
2. Add food coloring until you get the desired shade.
3. Mix with eggbeater until the paint has the consistency of whipped cream.
4. Paint away with fingers, feet or a large paintbrush.

Try This:

- Make a print. Place paper over the painting and gently press down. Remove to transfer the painting.
- Cover a painting with crumpled up cellophane wrap, foil, waxed paper, plastic bag, bubble wrap, foam egg carton or a string of beads. Allow to dry overnight. Remove carefully in the morning for an unusual texture.

Food Paint

K-3     

A mushy, satisfying experience!

Materials:

yogurt, ketchup, whipped cream, oatmeal, cream of wheat, pudding, gelatin
large, plastic tablecloth
heavy paper or cardboard

Process:

1. Provide the medium and let children embark on a sensory experiment.
2. Create for creation's sake–don't try to keep these works of art!

Try This:

- Paint right on a table.
- Open up plastic garbage bags for a large plastic tablecloth.
- Experiment with adding pigments to these paints.

Puddle Paint

K-3   

Single servings of finger paint offer a rich tactile and visual experience.

Materials:

1/2 cup (125 ml) liquid starch
powdered or liquid tempera paint
heavy paper

Process:

1. Pour a puddle of liquid starch on paper.
2. Sprinkle a teaspoon of paint in the middle of the puddle.
3. Artistic fingers and hands do the mixing.

Try This:

- Freezer paper makes great inexpensive finger paint paper. Use the shiny side.
- Introduce new vocabulary–swirling, spreading, mixing, deepening, lightening and blending.
- Moisten the paper lightly with a damp sponge before using.
- Experiment with adding pigments to these paints.

Easy Finger Paints

K-3

Materials:

3 T (45 ml) sugar
1/2 cup (125 ml) cornstarch
2 cups (500 ml) cold water
food coloring
1/4 cup (60 ml) liquid
washing detergent
4 cups
saucepan
spoon

Process:

1. Mix sugar and cornstarch together in the saucepan.
2. Add the water and stir as much as you like.
3. Put the saucepan over a burner on medium heat and stir constantly until the mixture comes to a boil.
4. Keep stirring until the paint mixture is thick and clear–about 6 minutes.
5. Remove from the element and cool for 5 to 15 minutes.
6. Pour the cool mixture into cups.
7. Add a little food coloring and a drop of detergent to each cup and stir until the paint is well blended.

Try This:

- Make a finger painting tray to keep the finger painter's work in place. Use the base of a cardboard box cut to have a 3/4" lip on all sides.
- Give students four small painting papers–have them number these. Play four musical selections (classical, children's pop, rhythm and blues and rock perhaps), and have students finger paint in the corresponding numbered paper to express the music.
- Set up a center with the various finger paints. Have students evaluate each one as they observe differences in texture and color. Follow up by graphing their conclusions.

Recycled Finger Paint

K-3 

Environmentally friendly smearing fun!

Materials:

- 1/2 cup (125 ml) discarded soap chips
- 1 cup (250 ml) cornstarch
- 6 cups (1500 ml) water
- large saucepan
- large mixing spoon
- grinding stone
- ladle
- stir sticks
- colored chalk ends or ground natural pigment
- individual storage containers with lids and labels

Process:

1. Put chalk and soap chips in separate bags.
2. Break soap chips into fine pieces on the grinding stone.
3. Combine soap chips, cornstarch and water in the pan.
4. Bring the mixture to a boil over medium heat and stir constantly until the mixture thickens.
5. Remove the mixture from the heat and pour into individual containers.
6. When the mixture is warm, students can mix one color of crushed chalk to each container.
7. Let cool and store in covered, labelled containers.

Try This:

- Provide a table full of interesting items for students to experiment in the paint with: combs, toothbrushes, coins, balls, jacks, marbles, toy cars, feathers, rubber stamps, paper clips, elastics, rings, washers, sponges, sections of fruits and vegetables, leaves, flower petals and more. Just ask for suggestions!

Face Paint

K-3  

This is just the thing when a class is ready for a new look!

Materials for Each Group:

8 tsp (40 ml) cornstarch
4 tsp (20 ml) water
4 tsp (20 ml) mild cold cream
food coloring
8-cup muffin tin
1 mirror
washcloths
mild soap

Process:

1. Split a class into groups for this activity. Provide one muffin tin per group.
2. In each cup of the muffin cup stir 1 teaspoon (5 ml) cornstarch, $\frac{1}{2}$ teaspoon (2.5 ml) water, $\frac{1}{2}$ teaspoon (2.5 ml) cold cream and 2 to 3 drops of food coloring–no more or the paint will be hard to remove. In the end there should be a different color in each cup.
3. The group members form partners, share the muffin tins and paint away.
4. Mirrors can enhance the facial artwork and encourage some dramatic play.
5. Students should wash up before going home. Supply some soft cloths and gentle soap.

Try This:

- Faces can be painted to complement a particular theme or dramatic presentation.
- Offer this activity with free exploration and experimentation. Try it again after viewing some examples and learning some face painting technique.
- The mixing in each cup of various quantities begs for a math lesson!

Foamy Fun Body Paint

An end-of-the-year-in-the-school-yard-with-a-sprinkler activity.

Materials:

bathing suits
towels
muffin tins
spoon
can of shaving or whipped cream
food coloring

Process:

1. Squirt the shaving cream into the muffin cups.
2. Add drops of various colors to each cup and mix with a spoon.
3. Change into bathing suits and meet at an outdoor location.
4. Use hands, sponges, cloths or paintbrushes to turn one another into works of art.
5. A few trips through the sprinkler, in the sprinkling skipping rope or under the hose will clean things right up.

Try This:

- Use several cans of shaving or whipped cream to create foamy multicolored sculptures.
- Have a Beard Day where students give each other creamy beards.
- Have students create costumes on one another to enhance a theme.

Camouflage Body Paint

K-3  

Materials:

dusting powder of cool, white ash or fine earth particles
clay, mud or ground charcoal
cloths, towels and gentle soap for cleaning up

Process:

1. Wear camouflage clothing or old bathing suits.
2. Cover exposed areas with a thin dusting of crushed white ash.
3. Cover dusted areas with clay, mud or cool ground charcoal. (If clay is used, dusting is not necessary.)

Try This:

- Play games where children try to blend in with their surroundings.
- Have children turn themselves into critters and creatures of the forest with this activity.
- Use this activity to teach children about animal camouflage techniques and the necessity for this.
- Investigate various aboriginal peoples around the world who use camouflage techniques for their survival.

Chapter 3

To Model and Sculpt

Something to Sink Your Hands Into

There's nothing quite like digging your hands into soft gooey stuff and making something. Homemade play doughs and clays are simple to make, easy to work with, kind to the environment and you won't have to raid the school coffers to get them.

There are formulas for many types of modeling goo from the soft, squishy, smelly kinds to the types that will harden to become permanent works for children to keep.

Play dough offers a medium for children to expand their abilities. It invites imaginative play, fine motor skill development, intellectual development, an early understanding of physics concepts, hand-eye coordination and social skills if group activities are undertaken. Play dough seems to have a soothing effect on students who spend time poking, flattening, rolling and squeezing.

Try out these neat doughs and clays to find the stuff you like to squish around with best. Students can experiment with ingredients and colors to invent their own formulas. They will find that the magic of creating these blobs is as much fun as using them.

There is a whole world waiting to get out of that blob of goo (easy, expressive)!

Aims:

- To create a wide variety of molding media.
- To utilize a wide range of modelling media to express oneself in individual works of art.

Objectives:

- Child will develop skill in manipulation of modelling and sculpting materials.
- Child will extend aesthetic sense through manipulation of modelling materials.

Tips and Tricks:

- Educators should handle the alum powder. If you do not need to store your dough, this can be eliminated from recipes.
- If you want to keep your dough or clay soft for a time, store it in a recycled plastic container or plastic bag securely tied closed.
- If your play dough smells a little funny or is growing hair, it's time to toss it out.
- Play dough will keep longer in the fridge, but it will take a moment to warm up . . . hand heat works great!
- The only tools you really need are your hands. Shape coils, balls and cylinders. Flatten them into boxes, pancakes and ribbons. These basic shapes can be made in all sizes and variations to create almost anything you want.

Make-in-a-Minute Dough

K-3  

This is the easiest play dough to make. It's fast and simple, and the ingredients are always on hand. It is very soft for little hands to work; it won't hurt a child who eats some by mistake!

Materials:

- 3 cups (750 ml) flour
- 1/2 cup (125 ml) salad oil
- 1/2 cup (125 ml) water
- food coloring

Process:

1. Add food coloring to the water until the right shade is achieved.
2. Use spoons and hands to mix flour, oil and enough colored water to turn this messy blob into a ball.
3. Knead the ball well and it's ready to use.
4. Store in airtight containter.

Try This:

- Different colors allow for all kinds of possibilities. Make several colors at once. Create your own colors.
- Use diagrams to illustrate kneading techniques.
- Allow kids to mess around with this dough without any instructions. Once they have explored all of their possibilities, you can sink your hands in and demonstrate rolling dough, rolling a "snake," making balls, marking using tools, poking with tools, shaping with cutters, folding, etc.
- Observe how a child manipulates the dough. Can the child pound, break up, stick to other surfaces, roll, flatten, pinch, squeeze, press, stroke, pat . . . ?

No-Cook Salt Dough

K-3  

No fuss, no muss, no heat and this recipe lasts a long time.

Materials:

1 cup (250 ml) white flour
1/2 cup (125 ml) salt
3 T (45 ml) vegetable oil
1 tsp (5 ml) alum (available at drugstores)
1/2 cup (125 ml) water (may not all be needed)

Process:

1. Stir all ingredients together.
2. Add a little or a lot of food coloring to the water.
3. Add small amounts of colored water (about a spoonful at a time) until the mixture looks like play dough.
4. Store in an airtight container or plastic bag.

Try This:

- Encourage kids to mix colors to create ones you don't have.
- Offer the dough on its own so kids can explore only the dough.
- Offer interesting tools later to teach manipulation of instruments. Let children explore the tools without imposing preconceived notions of how they should be used.
- Create interesting shapes and designs with the following things found around the house–forks, knives, spoons and other utensils, toothbrushes, cloth, wood, shoe soles, toy blocks, cookie cutters, screwdrivers, soap holders, toothpicks, sharp pencils and thread.
- Press dough through a garlic press for neat hair, string, spaghetti, squiggles, worms.
- Observe to see if the child begins to name textures, shapes and tools.

Magic Lump

K-3  

Turn a mess into the best fun around. This version lasts a long time.

Materials:

1 cup (250 ml) white flour
1/3 cup (80 ml) salt
2 tsp (10 ml) food coloring
1 T (15 ml) vegetable oil
2 T (30 ml) cream of tartar
1 cup (250 ml) water
plastic bag or airtight container

Process:

1. Mix all ingredients together in a saucepan over low-medium heat for about 5 minutes.
2. Stir until the mixture forms a lump in the middle of the pot.
3. Dump the hot blob onto a floured surface.
4. When the blob is cool enough–squish it, punch it and knead it.
5. Store in an airtight container in a cool place–preferably a refrigerator.

Try This:

- Discuss play dough with your class. What makes it great? What makes it a flop? Provide samples of the various doughs for students to rate.
- Diagrams and the written word can be combined for this survey. Compile the results on a pictograph for discussion.

* Caution: Heat source.

Awesome Dough

K-3 

This easy, long-lasting dough is a delight to play with.

Materials:

1/2 cup (125 ml) salt
1 3/4 cups (430 ml) water
food coloring or tempera powder
2 cups (500 ml) sifted all-purpose flour
2 T (30 ml) salad oil
2 T (30 ml) alum (available at drugstores)

Process:

1. Boil salt and water until the salt dissolves.
2. Add food coloring or tempera powder for color.
3. Stir in flour, salad oil and alum.
4. When cool enough, knead until the dough has an even consistency.
5. Keep at room temperature in an airtight container or a plastic bag.

Try This:

- Substitute cornmeal or whole wheat flour for the all-purpose flour to achieve an interesting consistency.
- Allow yourself a spacious workplace that won't be disturbed by an active child. Add to the creations to make scenes, villages . . . worlds!

Smelly Dough

K-3  

An experience for hands and noses!

Materials:

2 cups (500 ml) water
1/2 cup (125 ml) salt
1/2 cup (125 ml) flavored instant drink crystals (See options below.)
2 T (30 ml) pure vegetable oil
2 T (30 ml) powdered alum
2 cups (500 ml) all-purpose flour
food coloring (optional)

Process:

1. Stir water, salt and crystals, cocoa or extract (see choices) in a large pot over medium heat.
2. When mixture comes to a boil, remove it from heat.
3. Use a wooden spoon to stir in oil, alum, food coloring and flour.
4. Use your hands when the sticky mixture starts to form a ball.
5. When the ball is cool enough to handle, roll it onto a flat surface.
6. Knead until smooth.

Note: Modify the basic recipe to achieve the scent and color of dough you desire. See the choices below.

Try This:

Berry: Add at least 1/2 cup (125 ml) of berry-flavored crystals to desired strength of scent and color. A few drops of food coloring can be added for brighter color.

Chocolate: Dissolve 1/2 cup (125 ml) pure cocoa powder into hot water. Increase oil to 1/4 cup (60 ml).

Lemon: Add 2 tablespoons (30 ml) lemon extract. Add yellow food coloring until the desired shade is reached.

Peppermint: Add 2 tablespoons (30 ml) mint extract and green food coloring.

Bubble Gum: Add 2 tablespoons (30 ml) anise extract and red food coloring.

* Caution: Supervise carefully if students will be around heat source.

Soap Clay

K-3 · 10 min.

Materials:

$1^1/_2$ cup (375 ml) soap flakes
4 T (60 ml) hot tap water
food coloring (optional)
hand mixer
large bowl

Process:

1. Add food coloring to water.
2. Mix soap and water in bowl.
3. Beat with mixer until the mixture has the consistency of thick dough.
4. Shape the clay into creations.
5. Let dry thoroughly–this creation can be admired or used as a soap.

Try This:

- Leave the soap clay white for wintry works. Create an entire snow scene with the class creations. Begin with snowballs and expand on the "snowy" limits.
- Make a blob or block. Let it dry slightly. Carve a sculpture using a plastic knife.

Bounce and Stretch

K-3  

Materials:

2 T (30 ml) white glue
4 T (60 ml) water
1/4 tsp Borax™ powder
food coloring
2 cups
stir stick or tiny spoon
airtight container

Process:

1. Add coloring and 1 tablespoon (15 ml) of water to cup and stir.
2. Add glue and let sit.
3. In the other cup, add borax to 3 tablespoons (45 ml) of water. Stir until completely dissolved.
4. Stir the borax mixture constantly as you add the glue mixture.
5. Dump the rubbery blob onto a flat surface.
6. Knead until slippery and pliable.
7. Squish, squeeze, sculpt and bounce it!
8. Store in an airtight container for up to one week.

Try This:

- Stretch a ball of this dough over a colored comic or newsprint picture, press firmly and remove. This will pick up the picture which can be stretched into funny forms and faces.
- Play catch with a friend.
- An extra teaspoon of starch will make this more rubbery.
- You can work in a little water if this starts to dry out.

* Caution: Do not allow children to handle Borax™.

Creator's Clay

For permanent works.

Materials:

- 4 cups (1000 ml) baking soda
- 1 cup (250 ml) cornstarch
- 1 1/4 cups (310 ml) cold water
- saucepan
- spoon
- rolling pin
- baking tray
- cookie cutters
- straw
- sealer and/or paint
- sealed container

Process:

1. Mix baking soda and cornstarch in saucepan.
2. Add water and cook over medium heat, stirring constantly.
3. When mixture is the consistency of moist mashed potatoes, dump it onto a plate.
4. Cover with a damp cloth until cool enough to handle.
5. Gently pat until it is a smooth ball.
6. Put in a sealed container for 24 hours before using.
7. Store in a sealed container in a refrigerator–bringing to room temperature before use.
8. Form shapes or roll to about 1/4" (.6 cm) in thickness and cut with cookie cutters. If you want a hole, remember to do it while the dough is still soft. Use the straw.
9. Allow to air-dry or bake in a 200-250°F (93-121°C) oven for 2 to 3 hours until thoroughly dry.
10. Paint and/or seal when cool.

Try This:

- Make decorations, jewelry, badges, buttons.
- Make marbles and then play with them in the school yard.
- Pasta, acorns, sand or other art materials may be added to create an interesting effect.
- Put a straw through your creation before it dries to make a hole for thread, string or ribbon to hang your piece as a necklace or decoration.
- Baked or dried pieces can be glued to beds, dressers, door frames, window frames, treasure boxes, with an adult's help and a glue gun.
- Most doughs can be frozen and defrosted. Bring the clay to room temperature before using, or it will be difficult to work with.

Cinnamon Clay

K-3     

Materials:

1 cup (250 ml) cinnamon
1/4 cup (60 ml) white glue
1/4 to 1/2 cup (60 to 125 ml) water
ornament hooks or string
rolling pin
cookie cutters
straw
ribbon

Process:

1. Preheat oven to 200°F (93°C).
2. Mix all ingredients together in a large bowl.
3. Mix with hands until a nice soft ball forms.
4. Roll the ball on a flat surface using a rolling pin. Roll the clay until it is as thick as your finger.
5. Shape or cut with cookie cutters to make ornaments.
6. Poke a hole through each ornament with a straw or pencil.
7. Place the ornaments in a warm oven. Turn them every 5 to 10 minutes.
8. When they are firm, take them out to cool.
9. Place a ribbon through the hole and tie in a knot or bow so the creation can be hung somewhere for all to see.

Try This:

- Experiment with nutmeg, cloves and other spices.
- Almost any cylindrical object can be substituted for a rolling pin. Anything that rolls the dough out flat will do the trick. Incorporate a geometry lesson into a search for substitute rolling pins.

Bread-Rock Dough

K-3  

Bakes hard as a rock. Save your teeth; don't take a bite!

Materials:

4 cups (1000 ml) all-purpose flour
1 cup (250 ml) salt
$1^1/_2$ cups (375 ml) cold water
2 T (30 ml) white liquid soap
paper clips

Process:

1. Combine flour and salt in a large bowl.
2. Mix water and soap in a separate bowl; then pour over flour.
3. Stir quickly to combine.
4. Knead dough with hands until it is smooth.
5. Line a rimmed baking sheet with foil.
6. Shape handfuls of dough into creations. Tiny bread loaves, buns and creatures are only a beginning.
7. Bend paper clips around and press one end into dough to make hangers if desired.
8. Place creations on foil and bake in a 150°F (65°C) oven for 4 to 6 hours or until hard.

Try This:

- When creations are thoroughly dry, paint with acrylic or water paints. When dry, apply a sealer so they will keep for years in a dry place.

Edible Sculpture Dough

K-3  

No fuss, no muss, no heat and this recipe lasts a long time.

Materials:

1 packet dry yeast
1/2 cup (125 ml) warm water
1 egg
1/4 cup (60 ml) honey
1/4 cup (60 ml) sugar
1 tsp (5 ml) salt
1/4 cup (60 ml) margarine
1 cup (250 ml) milk
5 cups (1250 ml) flour
mixing bowl
spoon
cookie sheet

Process:

1. Mix half a cup of water with yeast until dissolved.
2. Separate the egg yolk and mix with sugar, honey, margarine and milk. Save the egg white for later.
3. Mix with yeast mixture.
4. Add salt and enough flour to make it firm.
5. Knead dough for 5 to 10 minutes and allow to rise for 1 hour.
6. Preheat oven to 350°F (177°C).
7. Form into shapes and sculptures and place on ungreased cookie sheet.
8. Whisk up egg white and paint it over top of the dough shapes.
9. Bake for 35 minutes in oven at 350°F (177°C).

Try This:

- Create theme-oriented breads and shapes.
- Make numbers, letters, even your name out of dough.
- Sculptures can be eaten or sealed for creations that will last for three months.

Sand Smush

K-3  

Materials:

2 cups (500 ml) sand
1 cup (250 ml) cornstarch
1 T (15 ml) alum
3/4 cup (180 ml) water
old pot
wooden spoon
newspaper

Process:

1. Stir sand, cornstarch, alum and water in the old pot until well mixed.
2. Put the pot over low heat and stir constantly until the mixture thickens to look like dough.
3. Take the pot off of the heat and let it cool.
4. When the messy mixture cools, model it into sand creations.
5. Let the sand sculptures dry at room temperature. Drying time will vary according to size of creations–expect anywhere from two to five days.

Try This:

- When the masterpiece is completely dry, sand it very gently with fine sandpaper. This will remove loose grains and give the piece a smooth look.
- Your creation can be painted–painting with a small sponge will give the work a marbled effect.
- Seal the finished creation with a finish of white glue applied with a paintbrush. (Other sealants include glazes, clear enamel sprays, lacquers or nail polish.)
- Sculpt characters and scenes from a story being studied in the classroom.

Sand Clay

K-3 

Materials:

6 cups (1500 ml) sand
1 cup (250 ml) white glue
water as needed
interesting containers
strong, flat surface for working
mixing bucket
stir stick

Process:

1. Mix glue and sand.
2. Add enough water to make it shapable.
3. Pack the mixture into containers.
4. Turn upside down and remove container.
5. Air-dry to harden.

Try This:

- For containers, try boxes, jelly molds, cans, cups, buckets, cardboard tubes, etc.
- Work as a group to create the best-lasting sand castle ever.
- Create an entire village with castles, trees, roads, animals, rivers, lakes, islands and more.
- Make flags on toothpicks ahead of time. Poke these into the sculpture before it dries.
- Make windows and doors by poking carefully with a tool of choice.
- When dry and hard, these creations can be painted.
- Are students able to problem solve to put the large shapes on the bottom of their structures?

Sawdust Dough

K-3   

Materials:

2 cups (500 ml) sawdust
1 cup (250 ml) flour
2 tsp (10 ml) white glue
2 tsp (10 ml) starch
large bowl
large spoon

Process:

1. Mix the dry ingredients together.
2. Moisten with starch, glue and water to gain a good modelling consistency.
3. Model around a wire or stick frame. Pat modelling mixture onto the frame, shaping as desired.
4. Allow creations to harden for a permanent work of art.
5. Finish with a coat of shellac or paint.

Try This:

- Ask students to suggest other possible modelling materials.
- Incorporate with a geography unit. Have students create raised maps or land structures, such as mountains, islands, continents, etc.

Gathered Natural Clay

K-3      

Materials:

clay deposit
sealed container for storing clay
bucket
smooth, hard surface
tools for digging
water

Materials for Tempering Agent:

grinding stone
any of seashells, pieces of brick, eggshells, old pottery

Process:

1. Research, inquire, ask local kids, gardeners or artists if they know of a good place to find a natural underground clay deposit. Kids enjoy seeking information regarding this form of "buried treasure." You might find a deposit at a building site, beneath grass and topsoil, but the best place to look is the banks of a creek. Get permission before digging!
2. Once you have found your clay deposit, gather it in a bucket with water.
3. Mush it and break up lumps with your fingers. Remove any impurities or debris.
4. Pour this "slip" mixture through a sieve.
5. Stir in a tempering agent. The clay should consist of 10 to 25% tempering agent. This will help prevent the clay from cracking, especially if the work is to be fired.
6. Let it stand for 12 hours.
7. Pour off the excess water.
8. Work the clay to get out air bubbles. Each student can repeatedly slam, pound, lift and turn the clay on a hard, smooth surface to remove any air bubbles and make it workable.
9. Shape the clay into sculptures, pots, bowls or other creations. Moisten or let the clay dry as needed to keep it pliable.
10. Keep unfinished pieces in plastic bags or sealed containers so they won't dry out.
11. Once you have shaped the clay into something you want to keep, let it dry thoroughly in a warm, breezy place with little temperature fluctuation and no moisture.

Gathered Natural Clay

K-3  

Process for Tempering Agent:

Crush and grind the material to a fine talc.

Try This:

- Use the clay to make pots, bowls, plaques, pencil holders, chimes, beads, etc.
- Natural clay can be yellow, red, brown or grayish color–let students explore the properties of these different clays.
- Study pot shapes of early peoples. How did they evolve? What are the benefits of various shapes?
- Make pots using a leaf-lined hole in the ground to shape the pot and hold it as you work.
- Shape the bottom of your pot by forming the clay around a pot or container. Build from this base up using clay coils or snakes. Work the coils together gently. To widen the pot, place coils slightly on the outside of the previous layer. To make the pot narrower, place the coils slightly on the inside.
- When the pot is formed but wet, etch designs or use objects to make interesting textures.
- When the work has dried to a leathery texture, rub it carefully with a smooth surface to give it a polished finish.
- A dried piece of clay work is called greenware. Investigate the processes involved in creating a finished piece of pottery.
- For a hard permanent piece, you can fire work. To make greenware into permanent clay pieces, a process called firing must take place in a very hot oven or fire called a kiln. A local pottery or art studio might allow you to fire pieces there.

Pulpy Plaster

K-3  

Materials:

4 cups (1000 ml) torn newsprint
water
1 tsp (5 ml) white glue
1 cup (250 ml) plaster of Paris

Process:

1. Tear newsprint into small pieces.
2. Add water to torn newsprint until you have a soupy mixture.
3. Let pulpy mixture stand in a bowl overnight.
4. Mix in glue and plaster of Paris until the mixture has a modelling consistency.
5. Form into creative shapes and sculptures.
6. Let dry at room temperature.

Try This:

- Add lightweight decorative items to the surface of the plaster piece before it dries.
- Encourage aesthetic appreciation by showing slides or photographs of famous sculpted works.

* Caution: Don't breathe plaster dust!

Chapter 4

Stirrings to Stick With

Collages, creatures, construction paper towns, all need that most important craft supply–good old glue. It need not be fancy if it does the sticky job of holding things together on the paper, the sculpture of the fabulous creation of any sort. Students feel a sense of accomplishment from making this very basic craft supply. A little dab will do it with these easy glues that can be made right in the classroom.

Aims:

- To create a wide variety of glues.
- To utilize a wide range of glues to allow expression of oneself in individual works of art.

Objectives:

- Child will assist in the making of a variety of glues.
- Child will develop skill in manipulation of glues, gluing tools and gluing techniques.
- Child will gain expertise in creating works by sticking objects together.
- Child will perceive and plan projects that will use a sticking substance.

Skill Development:

- Intellectual
- Emotional
- Language
- Social
- Fine Motor

Curriculum Links:

- Language
- Science
- Physical Education
- History
- Math
- Art
- Drama
- Geography

Tips and Tricks:

- It is a good idea to cover a work area when glue is involved. Although most glues wash up, some are harder than others to remove from surface. It is much easier to just roll up the newspaper and be free from the cleaning job. Some glues are worse than others.
- A smock or paint shirt will keep young artists glue-free.
- If you use your finger as a glue stick, before you know it your work will get sticky and muddled. Use a tool! A glue stick can be just about anything from a craft stick, a paintbrush, a stick or a cotton swab to a factory-made, bendable, plastic glue stick.
- Liquid starch makes a good paste for light papers.

Homemade Glue

K-3 

Materials:

3/4 cup (180 ml) water
2 T (30 ml) corn syrup
1 tsp (5 ml) white vinegar
1/2 cup (125 ml) cornstarch
3/4 cup (180 ml) water

Process:

1. Bring 3/4 cup (180 ml) water, corn syrup and 1 teaspoon (5 ml) white vinegar to a full rolling boil.
2. In another bowl, mix together cornstarch and 3/4 cup cold water.
3. Slowly add the cornstarch mixture to the hot mixture, stirring constantly.
4. Let stand overnight before using.

Try This:

- Glue layers of tissue paper one on top of the other as each dries over various objects to form "stained glass" works of art. Plastic bottles and interesting boxes become treasures!
- Make a collage of a collection. Use glue to show off items.

Papier-Mâché Paste

K-3

Materials:

newspaper
1 cup (250 ml) flour
3 cups (750 ml) water
saucepan
wooden spoon

Process:

1. Soak newspaper in bucket overnight. Squeeze out excess water.
2. Place flour in saucepan and gradually add water. Heat the mixture, stirring constantly to prevent lumps.
3. Boil for 5 minutes, stirring constantly until it thickens to a creamy consistency.
4. Let the mixture cool.
5. Tear paper (newsprint, newspaper, tissue paper or rice paper) into strips.
6. When the mixture is cool, the strips can be coated with it–by dipping and wiping.
7. Coat strips and mold around forms such as balloons, wooden frames, wire shapes, cardboard tubes, boxes or plastic bottles one layer at a time.
8. Let one layer dry completely (approximately 24 hours, depending upon the form), and then add another layer.
9. Add 6 or 7 layers to create a solid, interesting sculpture.

Try This:

- Sculpt with paper by squeezing and building a design or shape.
- Make a piñata for a special occasion. Cover a balloon in layers of paper and paste. When all layers have dried, pop the balloon. (Don't worry if it breaks along the way, after the first layers have dried, it doesn't matter.) Fill a top hole with treasures and treats. Using a large needle, pull string through the top of the piñata so it can be hung. Let it dry until it is very light and hard. Hang it and allow friends to take turns batting it with a stick. It will break easily to spill the treats.
- Decorate your sculpture with paint, glue and glitter, tissue paper flowers, collages of stamps, magazine pictures, feathers or any neat thing that will stick to your creation.

Rice Paste

K-3 

A nice paste for any paper.

Materials:

- rice
- heavy aluminum foil or plastic
- hammer or rolling pin
- storage container with a lid
- saucepan with lid
- stove
- permanent marker
- $1^1/_2$ cups (375 ml) water
- strainer or colander

Process:

1. Place about $^1/_2$ cup (125 ml) water and $^1/_2$ cup (125 ml) rice into a container with a lid.
2. Cover and let the mixture stand for a week.
3. Drain off water.
4. Pour rice onto aluminum foil or heavy plastic wrap.
5. Crush rice with a hammer or rolling pin.
6. Pour crushed rice into saucepan with 1 cup (250 ml) of water.
7. Bring to a rolling boil, stirring constantly.
8. Reduce heat to simmer until mixture thickens.
9. Strain mixture with a colander or strainer over storage container.
10. Allow the liquid to cool and become the rice paste.
11. Store in airtight, labelled container.

Try This:

- For variety, add color to the paste and use for gluing collages of sand, grains or paper.

* Caution: Heat source.

Easy Flour Paste

K-3  

Can be used to paste any paper, but performs best as a papier-mâché glue.

Materials:

1 cup (250 ml) flour
2/3 cup (160 ml) water
bowl
spoon

Process:

1. Spoon a small amount of flour into bowl and add water.
2. Mix together flour and water until mixture is smooth.
3. Add more water if the mixture is too stiff or more flour if the mixture is too runny.

Try This:

- Papier-mâché can be modelled like clay. Students can use it to make beads, dolls, masks and puppet heads.

Rawhide Glue

1-3   

Materials:

rawhide strips or rawhide dog bone
water (enough to cover rawhide in pot)
old cooking pot
stove

Process:

1. Put rawhide in cooking pot.
2. Add enough water to cover rawhide.
3. Boil gently until rawhide turns into thick mush. Time will vary, depending upon size of rawhide.
4. Let sit until mush cools and thickens.
5. You can boil further if you desire a thicker glue, or add water if you desire a thinner glue.

Try This:

- Only a small amount of this glue is needed. It works best on natural materials.
- Make wreaths using sticks, acorns, nuts, seeds and other objects.
- Create small stick scarecrow people using this glue to hold together sticks for the body and decorations to bring the scarecrow to life.
- Investigate how other glues are made.
- Cook in a well-ventilated area to minimize odor.

* Caution: Heat source.

Crude Pitch Glue

2-3 

Materials:

tree pitch
tree pitch hardening agent:
  cool white ash, ground
  eggshell or seashell
grinding stone
tongs
heat source

Process:

1. Gather pitch from an injured pine, spruce, fir, hemlock, cedar, yew, juniper or tamarack tree. Look for sticky dark substance semihard or dripping from the tree. Collect it on a stick.
2. Grind hardening agent: ashes, eggshell or seashells with a grinding stone.
3. Using tongs, hold the pitch piece over the area to be glued.
4. Apply a heat source such as a candle to the pitch and watch it drip onto the surface.
5. Sprinkle with hardening agent to make the glue magically harden before your eyes.

Try This:

- Learn about trees as you search for and gather the pitch. Use a tree identification guide. Encourage students to observe and discuss details about the trees.
- Use the pitch to make a stick "log house" for birds.

* Caution: Be careful when using a heat source.

Chapter 5

Dyes and Colors

Colors of the Rainbow

Interested in turning a collection of old shirts, socks or hats into a masterpiece of nature's colors? Until the mid 1800s all dyes came from natural materials. All the colors of the rainbow can be found in plant parts and transferred to materials with a little lesson in dyes. Natural dyes produce subtle colors and are less polluting than synthetic dyes. Have students explore the school yard for color sources. Put those dandelions to good use! Some dye sources can be bought at the market or found in the gardens of students.

Aims:

- To explore colors and means to transfer these colors to fabrics.
- To investigate plants as sources of color.

Objectives:

- Child will develop an appreciation for subtlety of color.
- Child will recognize various plants and their use as a dye source.
- Child will gain experience in a variety of dyeing processes.
- Child will become familiar with the terms and processes of transferring color to materials.
- Child will acquire skill in making and using dye baths which will give several colors to various materials.

Skill Development:

- Intellectual
- Emotional
- Language
- Social
- Fine Motor

Curriculum Links:

- Language
- Science
- Geography
- Health
- Math
- Art
- History
- Physical Education

Dye Source Color Chart

There are various field guides available to help with plant identification. Plants listed below are surprising sources of color. The colors given are an approximation of dye results. The more plant you use, the deeper the color will be.

Plant	Part	Color
blue lupine	flowers	pale green
broom	flowers	peach
Celandine	flowers	yellow
crocus	flowers (purple)	blue-green
daffodil	petals	yellow
dahlias	flowers	burnt orange
dandelion	flowers	bright yellow
goldenrod	flower heads	yellow, beige, gold
heather	flower tips	green
marigold	flower heads	brass
Queen Anne's lace	flower and stalk	pale yellow
sunflower	flowers	soft yellow
tansy	flowers	yellow
wild rose	hips	oatmeal brown
yarrow	flowers	light green/yellow
zinnias	flowers	burnt orange
agrimony	leaves and stalk	peach
beet	leaves and roots	pinkish green
birch	leaves	beige
broccoli	stalks	green
cabbage (purple)	leaves	blue-lavender
carrot	tops	yellow
comfrey	leaves	yellow
elderberry	leaves	beige
grass	leaves	green
hyssop	leaves	dark green
lamb's quarters	leaves	yellow green
lily of the valley	leaves	spring green
mullein	leaves and stalk	green
parsley	leaves	light green
peach	leaves	beige
pear	leaves	beige
plum	leaves	beige
poplar	leaves	orange/gold
rhododendron	leaves	beige
smartweed	all but roots	yellow-green
spinach	leaves	green

Dye Source Color Chart

Plant	Part	Color
stinging nettle	all but roots	light brown
sumac	leaves	browns
tea	leaves	light brown, rose, tan
alkanet	roots	brown
beet	root	gold, pinkish/green (let stand 2 days in half vinegar, half water salt rinse)
bloodroot	roots	dusty rose
dandelion	root	blue/gray
water lily	root	brown
blackberries	berries	purple/blue
blueberries	berries	deep blue
cranberries	berries	red
elderberries	berries	lavender
juniper mistletoe	berries	purple/gray
purple grape	fruit	wine
raspberries	berries	burgundy
rose hips	berries	red/pink
wild holly	berries	pale pink
apple	inner bark	light brown no mordant
birch	inner bark	light brown no mordant
hemlock	inner bark	light brown no mordant
oak	inner bark	brown no mordant
walnut	inner bark	light brown no mordant
black walnut	shells	dark brown no mordant
bracken fern	curled head	yellow green
coffee	beans	yellow tan
fenugreek	seeds	yellow brown
lichens		soft beiges and browns to pinks (soak in vinegar)
red onion	skins	mirky green
red clay	surface water	red
yellow onion	skins	light brown, burnt orange, yellow

Natural Dyes

Many natural materials from the yard or garden can be used to create subtle dyes.

Materials:

dye source material (see list)
large cooking pot (stainless steel glass or enamel) with lid
8 cups (2000 ml) soft water
stove
storage containers with lids
wooden spoon
colander or strainer
large mixing bowl
cotton string, natural wool or a cotton T-shirt
rubber gloves (to protect from heat and staining)
apron (to protect clothing)
Mordant (for 1 lb of material)
4 ounces (113 g) alum
2 T (30 ml) cream of tartar
4 gallons (15.12 l) soft or distilled water

Process:

1. Gather roots, berries, barks, flowers, leaves and plants in the following seasons:
   flowers: when young and vigorous, gather into a container of water. Handle gently.
   leaves: when first out in full (spring)
   berries: when slightly over ripe
   bark: spring from prunings or a felled tree
   roots: late summer and fall
   lichens: in damp weather
2. Break the plant pieces into small bits.
3. Combine the water and plant pieces in the pot. Do not use less than 1 cup (250 ml) of dye source material for a pint (.47 l) of water. More dye source material will make a stronger dye (1 gallon [3.78 l] boiling water/ 4 ounces [113 g] material to be dyed). Measure out the dye source material and water for the color you desire. Let the dye stuff soak in cold water for: bark–7 days; berries–1 to 2 days; flowers–1 1/2 hours; leaves and stalks–2 days; roots–4 days; spices, coffee and tea–no more than 1 hour.

* Caution: Work in a well-ventilated area–outdoors. Do not ingest dyes or mordant, as some of these may be toxic. Wash hands after handling materials or use rubber gloves as some materials are irritants.

Natural Dyes

K-3

Process:

4. Bring to a boil.
5. Strain the dyestuff material and resume boiling the liquid.
6. Cover dyestuff mixture with lid and bring to a boil. Continue boiling gently for about 1 hour, until water turns the color you desire. Stir occasionally.
7. Only a few natural dyes have good fastness to light and washing. Most require a mordant to fix the dye to the fabric. If the item is to stand up to washing, see Mordant below. Soak the items you plan to dye in fresh water or mordant–squeeze out excess water.
8. Add your items to the dye bath pot and simmer gently until desired color is achieved–about 1 hour. Wet fabric will look darker than it will once it has dried.
9. Remove pot from heat, leave items in dye bath to cool.
10. When cool, remove items from the pot, squeeze out excess water and hang or lay flat to dry.

Materials for 1 lb (40 kg) Mordant:

4 ounces (113 g) alum
2 T (30 ml) cream of tartar
4 gallons (15.12 l) soft or distilled water

Process for Mordant:

1. Add ingredients to the water in saucepan, stir and gently boil material for 15 minutes.
2. Add material and simmer gently for 1 hour.
3. Let material stand in liquid until cool.
4. Remove the item and squeeze out excess moisture. Dye the damp article or let dry and dye at another time.
   (A mordant can alter the color of the dye.)

* Caution: Work in a well-ventilated area or outdoors. Do not ingest dyes or mordant, as some of these may be toxic. Wash hands after handling materials or use rubber gloves as some materials are irritants.

Natural Dyes

K-3 

Try This:

- Enhance observation skills through a scavenger hunt for dye sources.
- Encourage students to experiment to find other colors.
- Have students guess and record what color they think each source will produce.
- Try tie-dye! Bind, pleat, fold, knot, twist, scrunch, crumple and tie with thin string before putting material in dye bath. Try wrapping buttons, marbles or other small shapes and tie tightly. Try dipping corners only. Let dry before untying.
- Try batik! Melt a wax of $1/2$ paraffin and beeswax. Paint a design on the fabric using wax and a paintbrush, toothpick, eyedropper or a cotton swab. Immerse in cold water. Add to the dye bath. Creates very interesting patterns! (For a simpler and safer but less effective method, draw on fabric with crayon, then dip in dye for a batik effect.)
- Incorporate with a study of plants. Consult an identification guide to help you find the right plant, flower, fruit or vegetable.
- Incorporate with a unit on native and pioneer peoples who used nature's colors to color the cotton, wool and linen fabrics they wore.
- Make a game of matching the dye source with cloth dyed by that source. Design a bulletin board to display the dye source and the cloth dyed by it.

Neat Things to Dye:

T-shirts
canvas shoes
paper
napkins
bathing suits
towels
school bags
marble bags
tissue paper
feathers
eggs

cloth swatches
shorts
pants
kite string
socks
hats
gloves
pillowcases
hair ribbons
bookmarks

* Caution: Work in a well-ventilated area or outdoors. Do not ingest dyes or mordant, as some of these may be toxic. Wash hands after handling materials or use rubber gloves as some materials are irritants.

* Caution: Heat source.

Kool Dyes

K-3      

Materials:

2 packages of unsweetened powdered drink mix
stainless steel, glass or enamel cooking pot with lid
1/2 cup (125 ml) white vinegar
1/2 gallon (1.89 l) water
stove
storage containers with lids for dyes (glass jars, plastic containers)
items to be dyed

Process:

1. Pour two packages of unsweetened Kool-Aid™ or powdered drink mix into cooking pot.
2. Add vinegar and water.
3. Cover and heat until pot steams.
4. Simmer for 20 to 30 minutes.
5. Let cool and pour dyes into storage containers or dye bath.
6. Soak item to be dyed in pot of dye until desired shade is reached.

Try This:

- Paint dye on fabric with brush or cotton swab.
- Dye napkins, place mats, bookmarks or paper for a school fund-raising activity.
- Purchase some indigo or madder dye at supply shops–these produce lovely colors.
- Incorporate a lesson on measurement and time, as needed for the recipe.
- Use pictographs to record students favorite colors.

Golden Eggs

2-3 

A traditional European onion skin dying method. Each egg will be different.

Materials:

cold water
12 or more onions, dark skins only
12 raw white eggs
small elastic bands
muslin
large pot
stove

Process:

1. Remove onion skins and soak for 5 minutes in a large pot filled with cold water.
2. Drain the skins into a colander.
3. Wrap 2 or 3 layers of skin around raw egg. Wrap in muslin. Fasten skins with elastic bands. A tie-dyed effect will appear where the elastic bands are fastened.
4. Layer eggs in pot.
5. Completely cover eggs with cold water.
6. Bring water to a boil over medium-high heat.
7. Reduce heat and simmer eggs for 10 minutes, partially covered.
8. Remove pot from heat.
9. Remove the egg and plunge into cold water.
10. Remove the muslin and onion skins.
11. Dry carefully. Refrigerate until needed in empty egg carton.

Try This:

- Rub with cooking oil for a shiny appearance.
- Use eggs for a centerpiece in a basket.
- Add other colors to egg with felt pens or attach transfers.
- Draw with white crayon on egg before dyeing for a batik effect.
- Hard-boil egg before dyeing to help prevent breakage.
- Experiment with a variety of natural materials to achieve a variety of colors.

*Caution: Heat source.

Resources

Evaluating a Child's Creative Progress

How does an educator evaluate a child's progress in a K-3 art program? Observe the individual child in a wide variety of art experiences. Focus on the child's growth and the process of creating rather than the end products. An exciting learning environment should facilitate the development of fine motor skills, language abilities, imaginative play, and social and emotional skills. A broad base of concepts and skills should be achieved during the various developmental stages.

Child three to five years of age will:

- participate with natural enthusiasm and spontaneity
- express himself freely
- manipulate materials in creative ways
- make use of found materials
- use language throughout an activity
- use tools in a manner limited by fine motor skill development
- use materials with a purpose
- become visually aware of details
- experiment with texture, form and color
- demonstrate a sustained interest in an art activity

Child five to seven years of age will:

- participate with natural enthusiasm and spontaneity
- express himself freely
- manipulate materials in creative ways
- make use of found materials
- use language throughout an activity
- recognize similarities and differences
- develop visual awareness of fine detail, scale, design, conservation, symmetry and color
- produce symbolic forms for a variety of familiar objects
- combine forms to express ideas, feelings or to tell a story
- demonstrate changes in intellectual growth through drawings
- combine materials in inventive ways
- demonstrate a variety of problem-solving techniques
- develop and use a growing art vocabulary
- participate in group efforts
- demonstrate a sustained interest in an art activity
- become self-motivated

Resources

Evaluating a Child's Creative Progress

Child seven to nine years of age will:

- participate with natural enthusiasm and spontaneity
- express himself freely
- manipulate materials in creative ways
- make use of found materials
- make use of advanced language before, during and after engaging in artistic activity
- manipulate tools and materials in a competent manner
- combine forms to express an idea
- make use of a rich art vocabulary
- demonstrate an increasing understanding of perspective, scale, proportion, profile, balance, design, horizontal and vertical lines, space, fine detail, design, color, texture, mood and motion
- develop a need for finer tools
- pre-plan works through discussion and sketches
- use art to communicate ideas
- integrate art skills with other subjects
- work well with others on projects
- demonstrate a sustained interest in an art activity

Evaluation of the Child

You may wish to use this checklist several times per child during the year. Date your evaluation so you can compare and note areas of progress.

Child's name ____________ Does the child . . .	Never	Some-times	Always
Make use of found materials?			
Use material with a purpose?			
Use art to communicate ideas?			
Experiment and manipulate materials freely in various media?			
Explore all the qualities of the media provided?			
Solve problems in an inventive manner?			
Produce a wide variety of symbolic forms?			
Use vocabulary that indicates artistic knowledge?			
Show attention to detail, color, texture, mood and motion?			
Demonstrate a working knowledge of the tools needed to create in the medium?			
Demonstrate the ability to organize and plan a project?			
Make use of a variety of techniques to create and complete works?			
Organize and present artwork in a creative way?			
Demonstrate initiative in art tasks?			
Work well in group projects?			
Incorporate independent thinking and problem-solving skills when creating a work?			
Demonstrate a degree of visual awareness appropriate to his or her age level?			
Demonstrate an increasing awareness of composition and detail?			
Make use of an understanding of arrangement, perspective, balance, scale, proportion, profile, conservation, symmetry, size of objects and use of space?			
Express ideas about the work verbally?			
Offer comments that demonstrate insight into various experiences?			
Complete given projects?			
Demonstrate progressive skill development?			
Demonstrate increasing appreciation of aesthetics?			
Show an appreciation of classmates' efforts and differences?			
Consolidate art skills with other subjects?			
Appraise his own work?			
Take pride in her work?			
Demonstrate a sustained interest and joy in artistic activity?			

Evaluation of the Artwork

Does the artwork demonstrate . . .

- originality?
- expression of personal feeling?
- good use of the media provided?
- an understanding of the skills needed?
- pride in work?
- a sense of harmony?

Cumulative art portfolios provide an excellent record of a child's progress and provide a base for discussion and evaluation.

Everything has its beauty but not everyone sees it.
Confucius

Evaluation of the Program

A sound art program should encourage creativity, stimulate language, develop aesthetic skills, enable plenty of experimentation, act as a vehicle for self-expression, reinforce a positive self-concept, aid in the development of physical coordination and lead to a feeling of joy.

Does the program . . .

- allow for individual creative expression?
- provide opportunities to manipulate and explore various media?
- offer developmental lessons with general direction and purpose?
- allow for the sequential development of the relevant art skills associated with the program?
- reinforce a child's positive self-concept?
- provide experiences which bring joy to the participation?

Scavenger Lists

Where Can I Find Free Materials?

Search, discover and recover! Prepare a letter to send home with students that lists the kind of materials your classroom could use. Let them know you collect "good" junk. Save packaging of all kinds. Enlist the help of local businesses, most have at least a little trash that could be put to good use in your classroom. Send out a letter stating your interest in their excess materials. Some businesses will even donate small samples of perfectly good stuff!

Check out your local resources with the eye of a scavenger! Here are a few suggestions:

interior decorator's business
floor covering store
hardware store
graphic arts studio
art supply store
local newspaper office
computer shop
school recycling bin
orthodontist's office
lumberyard
building site
fast food restaurant
grocery store
dry cleaning store
moving company
floral shop
feed supply store
garage sale
attics
craft bins
wall covering store
upholstery store
appliance store
framing shop
print shop
bookstore
electronic component shop
recycling center
doctor's office
woodworking shop
auto repair shop
cafeteria
food market
laundromat
airline company
garden center
local farm
thrift shop
junk drawer
basements

Try This:

- Provide shopkeepers and business owners with a large box that has your name on it, and ask them to save interesting scraps for you. Pick up your box once a month.

Materials Worth Scavenging

computer paper
wallpaper sample books
shredded paper
paper bags
frame shop mat scraps
old posters
used envelopes
used stamps
newspapers
magazines
cardboard
paper rolls
paper cups
junk mail
boxes
milk cartons
Styrofoam™ packing peanuts
Styrofoam™ trays
bubble wrap
foam balls
tin trays and pans
tinfoil
straws
stir sticks
craft sticks
rubber bands
carpet and flooring scraps
fabric scraps
quilter's scraps
thread
fabric samples
old clothing
buttons
odd socks
thread spools
shoelaces
string
yarn
twine
waxed floss
bows
ribbon
jar seals
pipe cleaners
marker lids
crayon stubs
candle stubs
beeswax
balloons
old hoses
puzzle pieces
plasticine
hardware
wood scraps
old paint
plastic bags
coat hangers
plastic tubs and containers
jars
crates
computer disks
computer chips
discarded computer equipment
electronic components
broken clocks
broken kitchen appliances
old telephones
discarded toys
old jewelry
old beads
fruit baskets
food containers
old signs
keys
flowers
straw
pennies
carpet and flooring scraps

Creations Bibliography

Bakule, Paula Dreifus, Ed., *Rodale's Book of Practical Formulas; Easy-to-Make, Easy-to-Use Recipes for Hundreds of Everyday Activities and Tasks*. U.S. Rodale Press, Inc., 1991.

Brown, Rachel. *The Weaving, Spinning and Dying Book*, 2nd Edition. Alfred A. Knopf, New York, 1983.

Burt, Erica. Illustrated by Malcolm S. Walker. *Natural Materials*. Bourke Enterprises, Inc., Vero Beach, FL, 1990.

Charles, Oz. *How Is a Crayon Made?* Simon & Schuster, New York, 1988.

Drake, Jane, and Ann Love. Illustrated by Heather Collins. *The Kids Cottage Book*. Kids Can Press. U.S. Distribution, Tricknor and Fields, 1993.

Erickson, Donna. Illustrated by David LaRochelle. *Prime Time Together . . . with Kids*. Discovery Toys, Augsburg Fortress, Minneapolis, 1989.

Fiarotta, Phyliss. *Snips and Snails and Walnut Whales*. Workman Publishing Co., 1975.

Graham, Ada. *Foxtails, Ferns and Fish Scales: A Handbook of Art and Nature Projects*. Four Winds Press, 1976.

Kohl, Mary Ann F. Illustrated by Kathleen Kerr. *Mudworks, Creative Clay, Dough and Modeling Experiences: Bright Ideas for Learning Centers*. Bellingham, WA, 1989.

Kohl, Mary Ann R. *Scribble Cookies and Other Independent Creative Art Experiences for Children: Bright Ideas for Learning Centers*. Bellingham, WA, 1989.

MacKay, Sharon, and David MacLeod. Illustrated by Marilyn Mets. *Chalk Around the Block*. Somerville House Publishing, Toronto, 1993.

Norris, Doreen, and Joyce Boucher. *Observing Children in the Formative Years*. The Board of Education for the city of Toronto, Toronto, 1980.

Palmer, John. *Drawing and Sketching*. Ron Ranson's Painting School Series. Anaya Publishers Ltd., Strode House, London, 1993.

Contraptions

Foreword

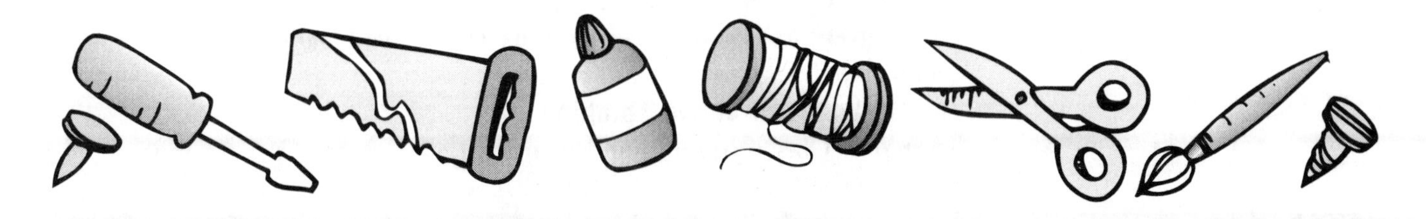

Kid Contraptions offers an exciting cross-curriculum approach to design and technology. This unique collection of do-it-yourself projects is geared to develop essential creative problem-solving skills by leading children to discoveries. Turn your space into an invention lab and watch children learn as they turn everyday items into original kid contraptions that really work.

Acknowledgements

A special thank you to the children who have shared their creative genius with me, especially Kiersten Eagan who shared her Just for Fun Inventions. For technical assistance, guidance, editing and enthusiasm, thank you to Peter Hunter (P.Eng.) and Charles Eagan (App. Math, E. Eng.). Special appreciation to the teachers and students of St. James School, Colgan and McNab Public School, Renfrew County who have shared their ideas and thoughts inventively with me. And finally, I would like to acknowledge the creative thinkers, all through time, who have approached life from a different angle and shared in the excitement of contraptions for the sheer joy of it.

Table of Contents

Chapter 4: Contraptions for Comfort 186

Chapter 5: Communication Contraptions . .197

Chapter 6: Just for Fun: Contraptions, Toys and Other Neat Kid Stuff 207

Resources 217

Symbol Key

These symbols will provide at-a-glance information regarding the preparation of the contraptions.

K, 1, 2, 3 Recommended grade level

Full child participation in preparation

Partial child participation in preparation

Caution, adult supervision required

Ten minutes of active preparation time

Ten to sixty minutes of active preparation time

Over one hour of active preparation time

Gift

Large space requirements

Creative challenge activity

Intensive project
Additional time, materials and assistance may be needed.

Good group project
Group interaction can be especially valuable in problem-solving activities. Foster idea acceptance and appreciation of one another's input.

Materials may be difficult to find

Safety

1. Provide students with clear, concise safety rules.
2. Follow instructions carefully.
3. Discuss the sensible use of tools, sharp objects, glass and equipment.
4. Provide ample, flat work space.
5. When necessary, wear a work smock, footwear, safety glasses, earplugs and rubber gloves.
6. Remind students to never put anything in their mouths, eyes or ears.
7. Check the safety of scrap materials. Avoid sharp edges or containers that once held items marked *Keep away from children.* Label all dangerous materials.
8. Always use permanent markers, labeled paints, glues, varnishes and other chemicals in well-ventilated areas.
9. Avoid accidents by maintaining a tidy work area.
10. Use your contraptions wisely. They may break and cause harm if they are pushed beyond their limits.

Aims and Objectives

Activities throughout this resource are designed with the intent to achieve general and specific goals as outlined here.

Aims

To provide the opportunity for children to:

- investigate their environment
- recognize a need for new products
- apply skills and knowledge to solve problems which arise from the needs of peoples and the Earth
- recognize and understand the science of why things happen
- understand how things happen by controlling materials and phenomena
- develop logical thinking and creative problem-solving strategies through a variety of relevant hands-on experiences
- use specific skills to design and make contraptions that will improve the world
- discover concepts and language of science, design and technology
- increase understanding and competence in an ever-changing technological society
- develop confidence in ability to creatively understand, interpret, design and create

Objectives

The child will:

- develop skill in thinking creatively and inventively
- practice various problem-solving strategies
- develop skill in handling various tools, materials and equipment
- be motivated to make discoveries about science and technology
- acquire technological concepts through active learning
- become familiar with the terms and processes of design and technology
- demonstrate an understanding of basic principles of science, design and technology
- develop an understanding of technological development and its impact on society
- use knowledge, skills and creative thinking to respond to a need
- design, plan, make and assess contraptions that really work
- become comfortable with using existing technology

Let's Get Inventive

What Is a Contraption?

It's a gadget; it's a machine; it's a makeshift kooky device that really works–it's a contraption! Contraptions are in themselves often valuable and useful and many a contraption was the beginning of a great invention.

Humans are always trying to make things better, stronger, easier, faster or more exciting. Contraptions have made it possible for humans to move heavy loads; send sound and images through wires and across airwaves; build tall structures that reach up, cross over (or under!) large bodies of water, move quickly from one place to another–even outer space!

Many of the things you use every day came from the creative mind of an inventor–like your toothbrush, your pencil, a doorknob, your computer–even your books! There are so many inventions around us that it may seem there is nothing left to invent. Not a chance–humans are always ready for a new gadget, tool, toy, game, computer program, robotic device, vehicle, process, improvement to an existing item or something entirely new. There is always the possibility of something that will make life easier or better–maybe something to help correct problems left by previous inventions!

Great Inventors and the Contraptions That Have Changed Our Lives

Hero was a famous, first century A.D., Greek engineer and mathematician who wrote books that discussed the lever, pulley, wedge, screw, windlass and the conversion of energy into useful means. He invented a toy called the Aeolipilé that worked by means of jet propulsion–it was the first-known steam turbine.

Archimedes (287 B.C.-212 B.C.) was a brilliant Greek scientist, who invented ideas and machines including the famous Archimedes' Screw.

Leonardo da Vinci (1452-1519) was one of the world's most remarkable inventors. His inventions were so far ahead of their time that the technology to build them was not available. His recorded ideas included flying machines, parachutes, a self-propelling car, a steam engine, a submarine, a paddleboat, a diver's helmet, machine tools and canals.

Isaac Newton (1642-1727): Newton's theories changed the way people looked at the world. He developed rules of calculus and his famous theory of gravity.

Benjamin Franklin (1706-1790): This well-known philosopher, scientist, American statesman and inventor proved that lightning was a discharge of electricity. His many inventions included an improved heating stove and the first lightning rod.

Richard Arkwrithg (1732-1792) was known as the Father of the Factory System. He invented the water frame in 1769, a fast-working cotton-spinning machine that could be left to spin by itself. Factories were built for this machine and the Industrial Revolution was underway.

James Watt (1736-1819) invented the first efficient steam engines to meet the need for power during the Industrial Revolution. Factories could work without water, horse or wind power. He coined the word *horsepower* to describe the power of his machine.

Edward Jenner (1749-1823) was an English country physician known as the Father of Immunology. He invented the first vaccine to prevent the deadly smallpox disease in 1796–an invention that effects health and disease control around the world to this day.

Thomas Edison (1847-1931) was one of the world's most successful inventors with over 1,000 patented inventions that changed life in the twentieth century. His inventions include the phonograph (the first record player), the kinetoscope (the first machine film projector), the stock market ticker, improvements to Bell's telephone and his most famous invention–the incandescent carbon filament light bulb.

Alexander Graham Bell (1847-1922) was a teacher of deaf people. His studies of sound led to his invention of the telephone, patented in 1876. This revolutionized long distance communication around the world.

Albert Einstein (1879-1955) was the most well-known inventor of ideas. His creative mathematical and scientific ideas changed the way scientists thought about the universe and gravity. He is well-known for his Special Theory of Relativity and his General Theory of Relativity. His theories inspired one of the major inventions of the twentieth century–nuclear power.

The Wright Brothers flew the first powered plane, near Kitty Hawk, North Carolina, in 1903, and air travel began to take off.

Presper Edkert, Jr. and John Mauchly (University of Pennsylvania engineers) co-invented the first general-purpose electronic digital computer the ENIAC (Electronic Numerical Integrator and Calculator) in1946. It could make 5,000 additions and 300 multiplications per second–the Computer Age was underway.

Marcian Hoff invented the microchip in 1971 at Intel Corporation in Silicon Valley, California. It was to change industry and information technology around the world.

Kids Can Be Inventors, Too!

Christmas Lights
A terrible fire in 1917 in New York caused by a Christmas tree decorated with candles led 15-year-old Albert Sadacca to invent Christmas tree lights. These didn't sell very well until Albert became the head of a multimillion dollar company.

Toy Truck
In 1963, at the age of six, Buddy Patch got a patent for the toy truck he invented and became one of the youngest inventors ever granted a patent.

Earmuffs
In 1873, in Maine, U.S.A., 15-year-old Chester Greenwood, bent wire into a headband, attached pieces of beaver skin to the sides and invented earmuffs!

Snowmobile
The snowy winters of Quebec led 15-year-old Armand Bombardier to create an unusual motorized sleigh using a car motor and an old airplane propeller and a sleigh. After some improvements to the original design, the snowmobile was patented in 1937.

Calculator
The mathematical genius Blaise Pascal (1623-1662) made the first calculating machine by the time he was 19. A series of gears and wheels and handles added or subtracted up to eight figures. Pascal went on to become a pioneer of hydraulics and pneumatics and set up a public transportation system in Paris using horse-drawn buses.

How to Foster Inventive Thinking

1. Create an atmosphere where children feel secure and free to explore, experiment and try out new ideas. Offer encouragement, praise, consistency and enthusiasm.

2. Provide a stimulating physical learning environment that offers inviting active learning centers and materials.

3. Allow children to help shape the learning environment by involving them in the planning of topics and the organization of the physical setting.

4. Provide a wide variety of experiences that will appeal to all kinds of kids. Offer a wide variety of instructional approaches that will encourage children to learn and create in a manner that best suits them. Provide the materials, then step back and let children investigate and explore.

5. Be prepared before starting an activity. Have materials and set-ups ready so your time can be spent facilitating true learning. Know where the projects are leading before you start and be ready with leading questions, new vocabulary and scientific explorations when opportunities arise.

6. Encourage an investigative approach. Stimulate children to observe, ask questions and use their imaginations, skills and senses to find out for themselves.

7. Lead children to discoveries by offering suggestions or asking leading questions at the appropriate times, such as: What do you think will happen? Why do you suppose. . . ? What did you do? I wonder if. . . ? How can we find out. . . ? etc. Encourage children to think out loud and praise efforts to solve problems.

8. Be open minded and flexible. Follow children's ideas and explanations and allow them to pursue the ideas that are most motivating.

9. Model enthusiasm and creative thinking.

10. Help children to enjoy discoveries and experience wonder.

Turn Your Classroom into an Invention Lab

Take advantage of children's natural curiosity by providing a stimulating Invention Lab. With the right attitude you can turn *anything* into an invention lab. All you need is an interesting array of materials, a little space to think, create and test inventions and an encouraging atmosphere! Give young inventors a rich array of hands-on activities that allow them to explore, examine, experiment and make new discoveries.

The program and environment should:

- allow for individual creative expression
- provide opportunities to manipulate and explore various materials and tools
- offer developmental lessons with general direction and purpose
- facilitate
- reinforce a child's positive self-concept
- provide experiences which bring satisfaction and joy to the participant

Design and Technology in Education

Design and technology provide relevant, active learning experiences that combine skills, knowledge and problem solving to create a tangible product that solves a perceived human problem or need.

Primary children can be introduced to information technology as a means to record, store or retrieve information. A computer can be used to store or provide information and to reinforce skills and concepts. The telephone or fax can assist in finding resource materials. Calculators can assist with calculations. Familiarization with various equipment will develop competence in the modern world and inspire innovations that will improve existing technology.

Creating Contraptions

The inventive mind is curious and persistent. Combine knowledge, culture, skills and attitudes about technological development, its use and impact on society into your curriculum. Challenge children to design and produce products that will improve the world in which we live. Children may help to create a better future for us all.

1. **Observe:** Is there a need that you can fulfill? Can you improve upon an existing method? Is there a problem you can solve with an idea, a process or a contraption?

2. **Brainstorm!** Think creatively. How can you solve the problem or meet the need?

3. **Research** and discuss your best solution.

4. **Get Started!** Make, plan and work out the details! How will you make your contraption? What materials will you need? Do you need assistance? Make lists. Think about form, construction, appearance, strength, economy, simplicity, safety and function.

5. **Make It!** Build your contraption and try it out. Learn from mistakes and remedy problems.

6. **Evaluate:** Does your contraption solve a problem or meet a need?

7. **Share It!** Demonstrate your contraption. Explain what it does and how it solves a problem or meets a need.

8. Congratulate yourself and move on to a new problem.

Basic Materials, Tools and Equipment

You can create most contraptions with inexpensive household materials, tools and equipment. You will need some basic tools to shape, cut and join various materials. Before you begin, put together a handy Inventors' Kit and a Creators' Corner.

Please exercise caution and common sense when using these materials with small children.

Inventors' Kit

The Inventors' Kit will help children design and build their unique inventions. Put together one large kit or, if your children are old enough, distribute one kit per group within the class. A plastic bin with a lid will work well to contain these items. Each group will assume responsibility for their materials and tools.

Simple Tools

scissors
marking pencil
paintbrush
hammer and nails
leather punch
screwdrivers and screws
wire cutters
craft knife
file
cool glue gun and glue sticks
metal ruler
sanding block
bradawl or knitting needle
junior saw
small vise
staplers of various sizes
mitre block
hand drill and drill bits
center punch
adjustable wrench
measuring tape
small vise that mounts sturdily to bench
carpenter's square

Basic Materials

marbles or ball bearings
wire
thread
paper fasteners
wood dowel
wood pieces of various sizes and shapes
masking, electrical, cellophane and duct tape
cardboard of various sizes, shapes and thickness
balloons
workboard: 15" x 18" (38.1 x 45.72 cm) of wood, thick cardboard or sturdy polystyrene
string
all-purpose and specialized glues
copper wire
new batteries
thumbtacks
safety glasses
rubber gloves
hinges
leather pieces

Enhancement Items

stopwatch
computer
level
paints

Creators' Corner

Collect a wide variety of scrap materials in a series of containers or an area known as the Creators' Corner. See "Materials Worth Scavenging" list for suggestions.

*Add interesting items to the kit and corner as your ideas and needs predict. Find safe substitutes if necessary.

Contraptions Lab Book

K-3  

Materials:

3-ring binder or duotang
paper
classroom reproducibles (optional)

Process:

1. Educator and children will discuss the concept of contraptions. Explain that the Contraptions Lab Book will act as a record of materials, ideas and working models relating to contraptions the child will create.
2. Each child will individualize a Contraptions Lab Book with their name and a drawing.
3. Child will keep a record of contraptions and related activities within this book in a variety of ways: written record, illustrations, diagrams, photographs, 3-D modeling on paper, reproducibles, etc.
4. Date each page to provide a history of the inventiveness process.

Try This:

- Develop skills in written communication, sketching and early graphing by using the Contraptions Lab Book.
- Make parents aware that this is a working lab book for brainstorming, independent recording and rough drafts. Include a page in the back for parental comments. The book can go between home and school as a form of communication.
- Encourage children to record their inventive ideas before and after the actual model is created. Keep the focus on the actual invention rather than on the record–especially with very young children.

Challenge:

As an inventor, how can you plan, record and save your creations? (Consider paper, recipe cards, chalkboard, 3-D models, oral stories, songs or rhymes, cassettes, videos or computer discs.)

- *Leonardo da Vinci bound his ideas and sketches together in special notebooks. In these books he used elaborate backwards writing that could only be read using a mirror. Why do you think he did this? To keep his ideas secret? For fun? To protect his ideas?*

Creative Challenges
Inventive Thinking Motivators

Every activity in this book offers a Creative Challenge geared to inspire the inventive thinking process needed for design and technology. Some activities are simply a Creative Challenge as will be indicated by the symbol . To make the most of these Challenges, provide opportunities for children to explore and express themselves in a way that best suits them: solitary or group investigation, hands on exploration, verbal expression, informative sketches, written record or a working model. Children of any age or ability can respond to challenges at their own level.

Try This:

- Prepare children to be receptive to the ideas of others.
- Model enthusiasm for others' ideas.
- Praise efforts to understand other children's ideas.
- Praise originality and inventive thinking–the more farfetched an idea the better!
- Make children aware that some of the craziest ideas have developed into great inventions.

I Spy

Materials:

Observant children

Process:

1. One child chooses an item within the other children's view. This item must be a part of a working invention in the classroom. This child says, "I spy with my little eye something that is. . . ." Encourage children to look for various pieces that make things work in the classroom, such as the long black arrow (that helps us tell time), the copper hook (that holds our coat) and the white cylinder (that is used to write on the board).
2. This child chooses others to guess the particular item.
3. The child who correctly guesses the chosen item takes over and spies a machine part and the game begins again.

Try This:

- Encourage children to think about the shape, purpose or action of chosen items.

I Can Make It

 K-3     

An exercise designed to help children gain skill in the basics of observing, planning, interpreting, shaping, joining and critical analysis.

Materials:

- pictures of gadgets and machines (photographs, posters, magazine clippings, etc.)
- variety of scrap materials: paper rolls, foam trays, egg cartons, thread spools, pipe cleaners
- various tools and creative materials: glue, tape, scissors, rubber bands, joiners, fasteners
- flat work surface

Process:

1. Set up centers that offer a variety of interesting scrap materials. At each center display pictures of various inventions, i.e. doorknobs, chimneys, toothbrushes, chairs, binoculars.
2. ***Challenge:*** Make a model of . . .
3. Children choose a center and look very closely at the object in the picture. What shapes do they spy? What materials will be needed?
4. Children make a model of the object using the scrap materials at their center.
5. Children may put models in a display if they choose.

Try This:

- Encourage students to look carefully at shapes in the picture and shapes of their scrap materials. Ask questions about similar objects that could be made with the particular materials.
- Discuss whether or not the child's model will work like the object in the picture. Why or why not? What might be needed to make the model into a working model?
- Take this opportunity to establish and record children's degree of competency with particular tools and materials and their ability to visualize possible outcomes. What extension activities would be appropriate for their level of development?

Keep It Together

 1-3  

Materials:

3' x 2' (.91 m) board of masonite or Plexiglas™
1 container filled with assorted materials: rubber bands, craft sticks, erasers, pencils
string per child or group
small block of paraffin wax

Process:

1. Set the board on a small incline of approximately 40° angle, that allows materials to "slide down the hill."
2. ***Challenge:*** The materials at the top of this large hill must travel to the bottom of the hill. The materials must stay together for the entire journey.
3. Provide each child or group with the challenge and materials as stated above.
4. Facilitate and allow time for children to discuss and plan, experiment, make mistakes and try again.
5. Have children demonstrate and explain their solutions to the problem.

Try This:

- Students who find a solution before others can be given an additional challenge. Provide them with a stopwatch, and challenge them to find ways to move the materials more quickly.

What Could It Be?

 K-3  

Materials:

containers of various shapes and sizes
record sheet
pencil

Process:

1. Put various containers with the same attributes at several centers.
2. Children proceed to each center with pencil and record sheet.
3. Children explore various containers and record what the container could be.
4. Encourage children to look at the container from various angles. Ask questions such as: Where do we see that shape? What can that shape be used for? Is there anything in your home that has that shape? Where do we see that shape outside?
5. Children record their ideas for later discussion with the group.

Try This:

- Try this activity using gears, hardware, wood scraps, plastic shapes, etc.

Make It Better

 1-3  

Redesign an everyday household item. You may build a better mousetrap!

Materials:

collection of everyday items: cup, pencil, broom, juice jug, telephone
pencil and paper
selection of "junk materials"

Process:

1. As a group, choose one item to make better.
2. Model careful observation and analysis skills. What does this item do? What shape is it? Why is it made this way? Are there any problems with this item?
3. ***Challenge:*** Make this item better than it is.
4. Encourage students to imagine an ideal item of this nature. What would we like to see it do? Encourage creative, farfetched, innovative ideas. Discuss how this item might be altered to become more like the "ideal" item as imagined by creative thinkers.
5. Assist children as they redesign the item through drawings and exploration of various concrete materials.
6. Provide materials and tools for children to make a "new and improved . . . ."
7. Allow children to present their objects to one another if they choose.

Try This:

- Ask children to bring an ordinary tool, gadget or household contraption. Improve upon these objects. This will help children to look at their own belongings with the eyes of an inventor.
- Take photographs of the improved objects and have children write explanations of their items. Put these photographs and informative paragraphs together in *The New and Improved Book*.

Patent Registration Form

Patent Registration Number: ______________________________

Inventor: ______________________________

Name of Contraption: ______________________________

Description: ______________________________

____

____

____

____

Photo or Sketch

Date: ______________________________

Signature: ______________________________

(Classroom Patent Registration Committee Member)

Associate Inventor Award

This award is presented to

____

in recognition of valuable contribution to the invention

____

Signed ____________________

Inventive Thinking Award

This award is presented to

____

for demonstrating outstanding inventive thinking skills.

Your questioning, observing and problem solving will lead to great things!

Signed ____________________

Chapter 2

Machine Mania

What Is a Machine?

A machine is the basis for all contraptions. It is a human-made device that makes a task easier. A machine helps us to make better use of force (the push and pull on an object that causes it to move). Some machines are small and simple like a pencil sharpener, that uses a tuning force to cut wood, or a bottle opener or a pair of scissors which use lever action. Some machines are large and complicated like cranes, trains or airplanes. Humans are the only animals to build machines, and we use them to do jobs we can't do by ourselves, like build skyscrapers, lift heavy loads or move us, sometimes faster than the speed of sound, sometimes all the way to outer space!

An automatic or smart machine can work under its own control. To wash your clothes, all you need to do is turn the dial or push a button on the washing machine. A calculator is a small very complex machine that helps you to solve math problems quickly with the push of some buttons. Robots are machines that are made to copy human movements. They can do the work of many people or do tasks that people find boring or dangerous.

Simple Machines

All the tools we use around the house are based on six simple machines: lever, pulley, wheel and axle, wedge, screw and inclined plane. Some machines are operated by hand; others are powered by engines or motors. A complex machine or tool consists of two or more simple tools. A pair of scissors is a complex tool consisting of two wedges held together with a screw. The handles act as a lever and force the two wedges through the material being cut.

More power to you! Use a machine to help you cut tin (can opener), lift a car by yourself (car jack), pull a nail from a piece of wood (curved lever, claw hammer), split apart wire (wire snips), tighten metal on metal (wrench), remove lids (screw), break apart wood (wedge, axe), move yourself and heavy things to high places (stairs and ramps) and move yourself quickly (wheel and axle).

Name ______________________________

Machines Are Everywhere!

Find and circle the machines in this picture.

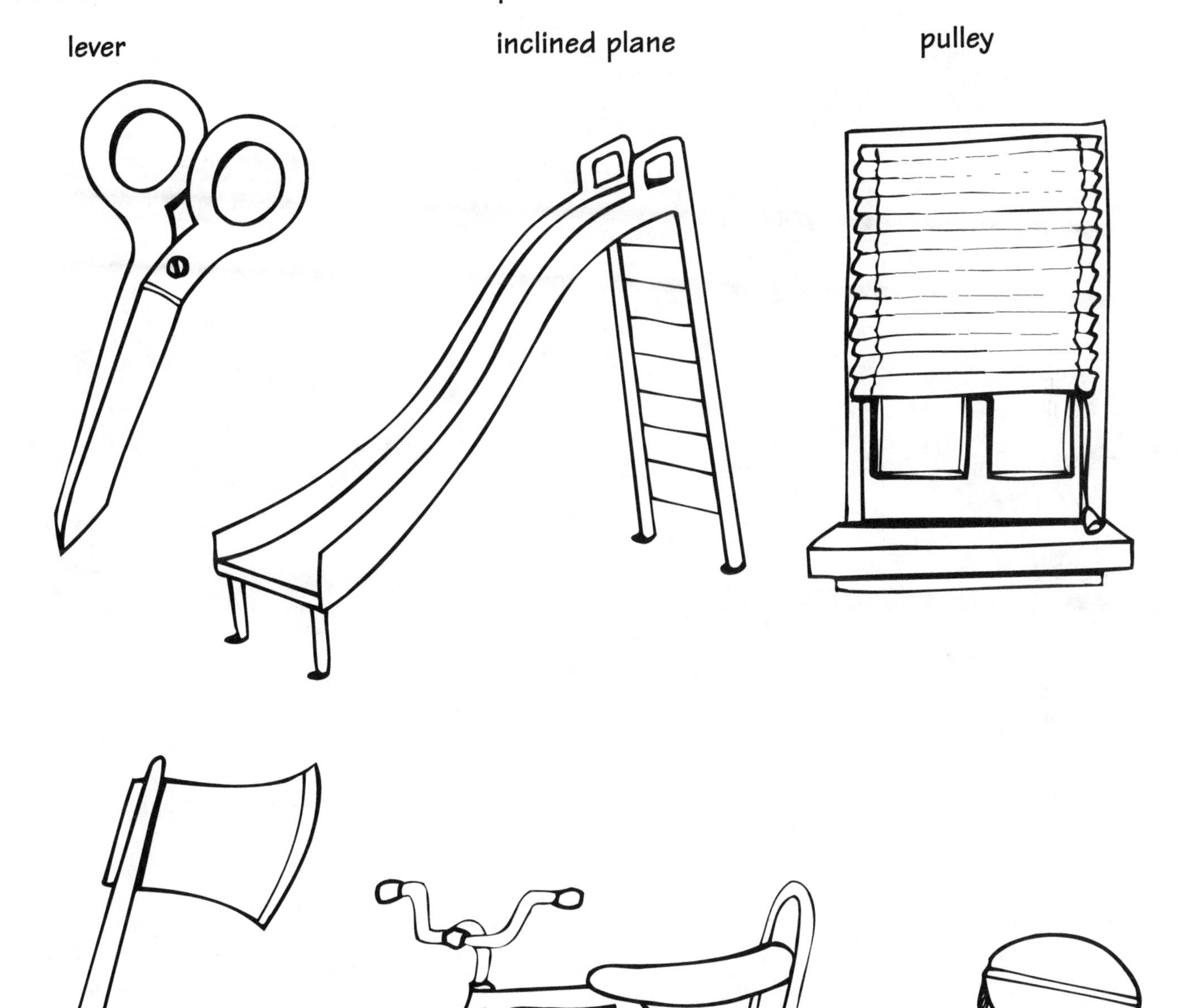

wedge

wheel and axle

screw

Machine Hunt

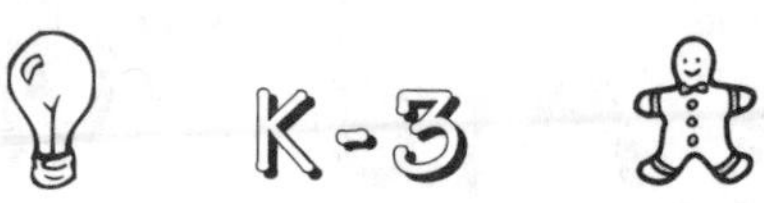

A great way to open children's eyes to the machines around them.

Materials: school, home or neighborhood
investigative, observant children

Process:

1. Introduce the concept of a machine as something that makes a task easier.
2. ***Challenge:*** Find as many machines as you can.
3. Take a walk around a home, school or neighborhood. Encourage children to look at small and large, simple or complex items.
4. Return to the class to list and discuss the many machines. This is a wonderful opportunity to make children aware of the attributes and various types of machines. Ask questions such as: How is that machine like the one Billy saw? How does that machine make life easier or better?

Try This:

- Can children identify what simple machine or machines are incorporated into the device? Think about the parts that do the work and draw that part.
- Photograph or sketch the various machines for a bulletin board display.
- Provide a Take Apart Center where children can take the covers off machines and look inside to see the way a machine works. Try a clock, pencil sharpener, electric car, etc.
- Research or make up a story about the inventor of a particular machine. What need was perceived? How did the idea originate? What was the first model made of?

Marble Maze

 1-3  

A contraption that uses all kinds of materials and all types of machines.

A **lever** is a simple machine used to make work easier by helping us to lift or move heavy loads with little effort or to act as a prying device. It consists of a lifting piece and a stationary or pivot point known as the fulcrum (i.e. the screw on scissors or the point where the hammer head rests on a board). Force on one end of a lever causes the other end to go up with greater force to lift a load, turn a bolt or pry into something. A clawed hammer and crowbar are simple levers, pliers or a pair of scissors are double levers.

An **inclined plane** is a simple machine that can be used to raise an object from one level to another with less force. It is a slanting surface that helps to move things up or down. Stairs, sloping floors and ramps are inclined planes.

A **screw** is a special kind of inclined plane that spirals around a center rod. It is used for raising things like the lid on a jar, piano stool or auger. It also holds things together in its common form as a wood or metal screw.

A **wedge** has a slanted inclined plane that ends in a sharp thin end. It is used for cutting and prying things apart. Knives and axes, scissors and needles are wedges.

Materials:

1 large low-sided box or wood frame
cardboard tubes, plastic tubes or quarter-round
wooden craft sticks
tape
creative materials: feathers, string, streamers, boxes, containers
scissors, craft knife or junior saw
glue, fasteners, staples, glue gun or hammer and finishing nails

Process:

1. ***Challenge:*** Design and make a maze to move the marbles from the top of the frame to the bottom, making use of inclined planes and a lever.
2. Assist children as they join and connect various tubes and paths for the marbles to travel down.
3. Recognize efforts to use an inclined plane or lever.

Try This:

- Tape or squeeze one paper tube inside another.
- Make a lever to catch and then lower a marble.
- Provide opportunities for children to experience various commercially made marble mazes. Talk about the motion of the marbles.

Shoe Racers

K-3

Recycled, inventive contraptions for hours of fun.

A **wheel and axle** is a simple machine used to move things. The wheel is a circle with a hub or center where a rod or axle goes through. The wheel rotates around the axle as you see with a rolling pin.

Materials:

old shoe
coat hanger or similar wire
bead spacers
thread spools
packing tape

Process:

1. ***Challenge:*** Using these materials, make a vehicle that can be raced.
2. Provide the materials and the Challenge and allow children to discover problems and solutions for themselves as they design and build their vehicles.
3. Encourage children to examine the materials and plan a vehicle before beginning. Drawings may be helpful.
4. Ask leading questions: Will the wheels turn? Does the vehicle need something to hold the wheels? How can we attach the axle? How will the wheels stay on the vehicle? How many wheels does the vehicle need? How can we test our ideas?
5. Introduce new vocabulary–wheels, axle, wire snips, spacer, rotate. . . .

Try This:

- Incorporate an art lesson. Make the racers sporty with decorations of all kinds–paints, stickers, ribbons, balloon bumpers, flags, fabric paints, neon headlights, etc. Be creative!
- Make a "driver" for the racer. Plush characters, plastic figures or paper personalities will bring the race to life. The cut off end of a balloon makes a nifty racing helmet.
- Make an inclined plane racetrack for the racers. Separate tracks with a shoelace lane marker hot glued to the track. Decorate the track with flags, toothpick and gumdrop stands and structures.
- Host a Big Race Day and set up a Sporty Racers display.
- Make a simple wheel by cutting out a cardboard circle and pushing a pencil through the center. Friction prevents it from spinning quickly.

* Caution: Be careful with wire snips and glue gun.

Challenge:

For advanced children: Make your vehicle go faster. Can you measure the speed of the vehicle? Provide a stopwatch and a means to measure and mark the track.

Gear Up

1-3  

Gears are wheels with teeth used to transfer force from one part of a machine to another. The teeth mesh, or fit together so one wheel can turn another wheel to make a task easier. Sometimes one wheel turns another with a belt or a drive chain like on a bicycle.

Materials:

heavy cardboard
(at least 3/8" [.95 cm])
craft knife
cutting mat
mounting board of cardboard
thumbtacks of finishing nails
compass to draw circles

Process:

1. Using pencil design and draw gears on cardboard.
2. Cut these on a cutting mat.
3. Mount the gears on a heavy sheet of cardboard so that each gear turns the next.

Try This:

- Introduce a tiny drive chain (of paper clips) to fit around the teeth, now called sprockets.
- Investigate the drive chain on a bicycle.
- Research the fascinating invention of the bicycle from the first pedalless wooden dandy horse in 1817 to the modern racing cycles of today.
- Investigate a hand-held eggbeater. Crank the handle and watch the motion transfer to two wheels that whirl in opposite directions to make a job easier.
- Look at the crank-operated pencil sharpener.

* Caution: Be careful when cutting.

Challenge:

Make one gear with ten teeth and one gear, half the radius of the larger, with five teeth. The teeth should be the same size on both gears. If the large gear makes seven revolutions, how many revolutions does the small gear make?

Thread Spool, Box and String Crane

2-3  

A **pulley** is a simple machine that helps lift things by increasing and changing the direction of force. It is a special grooved wheel turned by a rope or drive belt. A series of pulleys provides a mechanical advantage that allows work to be done with less effort.

Materials:

- 2' (.61 m) string
- 4" (10.16 cm) string
- hammer and two nails that are longer than the length of the spools
- tape
- paper clip
- 2 thread spools
- scissors, junior saw or craft knife
- plastic tub or other small container
- piece of wood
- cargo
- strong cardboard box (about the size of a shoe box)
- handle: dowel and wood strip
- 2' x 2' piece of balsa wood (about 24" [.61 m] long)

Process:

1. Mark and cut a hole in the box to snugly position the wooden "boom" so that one end is supported against the inside of the box and the other end protrudes at approximately a 45° angle, about 6" (15.24 cm) beyond the base box.
2. Temporarily position the "boom" and pencil mark about 1 1/2" from the base box up the "boom" and 1/4" from the end of the "boom" on the same side.
3. Remove the "boom" and nail one spool at each marked position. Ensure that the spool turns freely. Replace the "boom" in the hole.
4. Using the 4" (10.16 cm) string and tape, make a handle like that on a pail for the lifting container. Try lifting it. Reposition the handle if necessary.
5. Poke a pencil or small wood strip into the lower spool to form a crank.
6. Tape one end of the 2' (.61 m) string to the lower spool. Wind the string around the spool.
7. Bring the other end of the string over the top spool and attach a paper clip hook.
8. Wind the other end of the string onto the lower spool.
9. Fill lifting container with the cargo and hook the container to the crane.
10. Wind the handle and watch the cargo rise.

Try This:

- Discuss how a pulley can help to lift a heavy load as the upper spool transfers the downward force of the children's actions on the handle into the upward lift that raises the load.
- Add a weight to the top of the box or L-support if the need for counterweight arises.
- Put a magnet in place of the hook and watch the crane pick up the magnetic items.

* Caution: Be careful using tools.

Challenge:

Make a pulley. Provide wire, thread spools, string, hooks and heavy objects.

My Machine

1-3

Invent a new machine of your own!

Materials:

paper and pencil

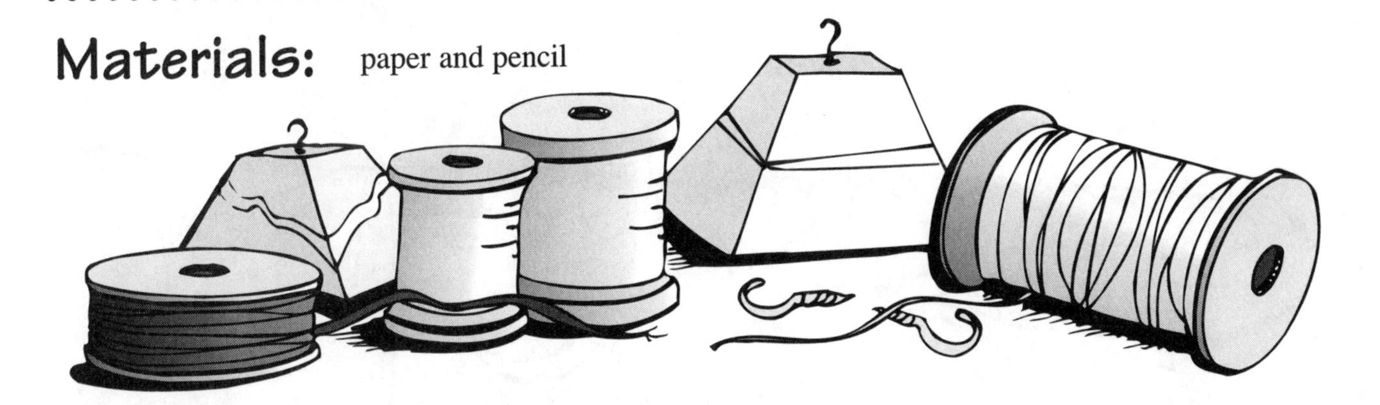

Process:

1. Discuss machines and inventions. Is there a need for something? A need to do something better, easier or faster?
2. ***Challenge:*** Design a new machine.
3. Name the machine and sketch and describe it in your Contraptions Lab Book. Explain what the machine does and what makes it work.

Try This:

- Present machines to one another.
- Make your machine with your Inventors' Kit and scrap materials. Take photographs.
- File a Patent Registration Form in your classroom.
- Make a bulletin board display of the machine designs. Add gears and pulleys around the border to make the display more interesting.
- Most machines help to make our lives better at the particular point in time. Discuss the ways that some machines have made the quality of our lives worse. Consider pollution and weapons.

Chapter 3

Energy Transfer and Complex Mechanical Machines

Make the most of your contraptions with energy transfer, the basis for movement in machines!

Potential energy, as is stored in our muscles or in fuels, allows us to apply force to move things. Potential energy can be transferred from these sources to make contraptions move in particular ways.

Many machines are powered by motors, complicated contraptions that change potential energy into movement (kinetic energy). Various mechanisms allow machines to turn one kind of motion into another and apply just the right amount of force in just the right place.

Energy Transfer

K-3 

Materials:

3 pencils
1 rubber band

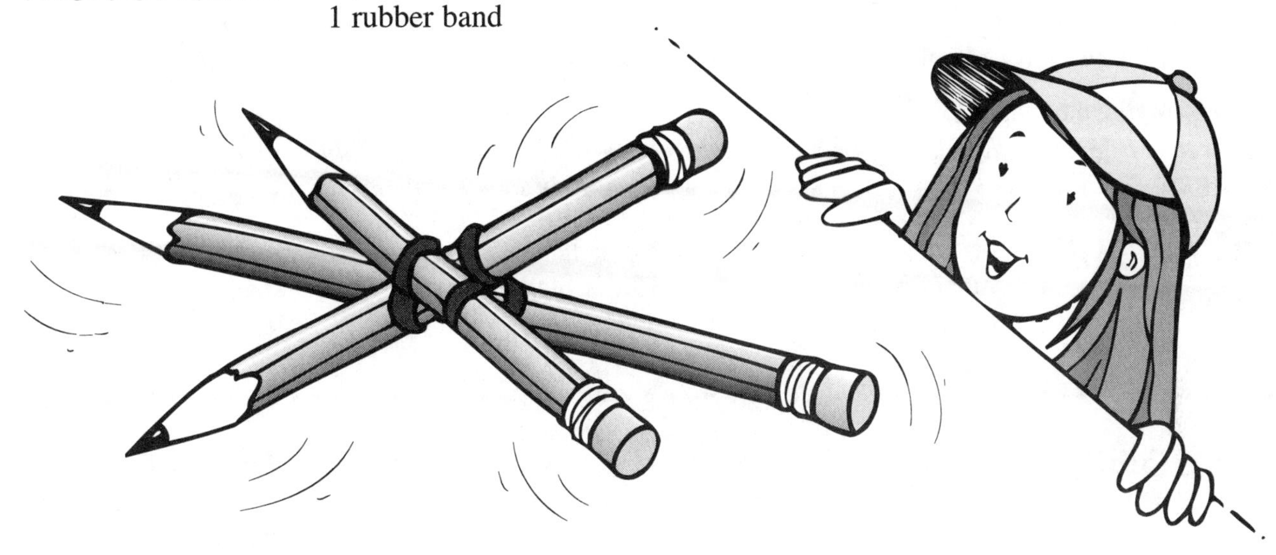

Process:

1. Wrap the rubber band around the pencils twice to make a snug fit.
2. Twist the pencils around and around, between one another twisting the rubber band.
3. Let go of the pencils and watch them dance. That's energy transfer.
4. Talk about how energy from your muscles is transferred to the rubber band. The energy you have used to twist the rubber band is stored in the band. When the pencils are released, the band untwists and the stored energy is changed into a flurry of movement that makes the pencils dance.

Try This:

- Find out about the various kinds of stored energy.

Challenge:

Make a contraption that stores energy to be changed into movement. Provide cardboard, plastic or tin tubes, cardboard end pieces, a compass, rubber bands and heavy buttons or nuts.

- *Many kinds of machines, including cars, contain their own stores of energy to change into movement. The energy for a car is supplied in the form of fuel that is changed into forward or backward movement.*

Friction Fighters

K-3

Friction: Whenever anything moves on Earth, it encounters a force of resistance called friction. Friction opposes motion and causes moving objects to slow down and eventually stop. It produces heat and wear and hinders the operation of machines. Inventors look for ways to reduce friction between the moving parts of a machine. Oil and ball bearings are used in various contraptions to reduce friction.

When you go down a slide, the force of gravity gets you going. Gravity also makes you accelerate as you go down the slide while the force of friction makes you slow down and eventually stop.

Materials:

book
rubber bands
paper clips
6 pencils
15 marbles the same size
3 jar lids of different sizes
table

Process:

1. Put a rubber band around the book. Hook the paper clip to the band on one end of the book.
2. Move the book across the table using the hook. Ask "How did you move the book?" Encourage children to talk about pushing or pulling the book–applying force.
3. Ask "Did the book move easily? What is preventing the book from moving freely?"
4. ***Challenge:*** Move the book using the lid, pencils and marbles.
5. Encourage all methods of movement. Ask "How does this motion feel compared to before? What else can you try? Why do you think that works?" Lead children to understand that rolling items reduces friction.

Try This:

- Investigate friction. Move things on rough and smooth surfaces.
- Rub two blocks of wood together. How do they feel? Friction produces heat.
- Friction produces wear. Look for signs of friction (shoes, erasers, paths, flooring).
- Wheels that move fast have ball bearings around their axles. Investigate the wheels of bicycles, automobiles, electric fans, food mixers and roller skates. Display commercial ball bearings. Discuss how ball bearings roll against an axle and cut down on friction. Listen for ball bearings in the wheels of a roller skate or skateboard.
- Provide 15 marbles the same size and three jar lids of different sizes. Put the smallest lid inside the middle-sized lid. Put a ring of marbles around the edge of the small lid and put the large lid over the top. Put a book on the lid and spin it.
- The first wheel was probably a rolling log. How could that have come about?

Safe Landing Contraption

K-3  

A contraption that tames the force of gravity with air friction.

Materials:

large square of cloth or plastic
4 lengths of string about 20" (50.8 cm) long
small light weight: cloth doll, plastic figurine or washer

Process:

1. Tie one string to each corner of your cloth.
2. Tie the four ends of string into a knot.
3. Attach a parachutist to the knot.
4. Hang the cloth from its center point.
5. With a swinging motion, toss the parachute into the air and watch it float back down.
6. Discuss the way gravity pulls the parachutist to the ground while air friction on the parachute opposes gravity making for a safe landing.

Try This:

- Parachutes can control their descent by using cords to vary the air flow in the parachute.
- Talk about another contraption that uses friction–brakes! The harder the brake presses on the wheel, the slower the vehicle goes. Test it out on bicycles.

Challenge:

Design another contraption that uses friction.

Old-Fashioned Waterwheel

K-3 

Materials:

water hose or tube attached to a tap
water center or outdoor space
PVC pipe (6"-12" [15.24-30.48 cm] long)
2 ice cream container lids
polystyrene trays
water-resistant glue (cool glue gun and glue sticks)
string or dowelling to fit inside the PVC pipe
set of compasses

Process:

1. Mark and drill a center hole to fit the PVC pipe on the two container lids.
2. Cut four 2" (5.08 cm) slats of polystyrene to fit from the center of the lid to the outside edge.
3. Mark the center of the PVC pipe.
4. Put one lid onto the PVC. Glue it 1" (2.54 cm) from the center line.
5. Glue the four slats, equal distances apart, to the lid and the PVC pipe.
6. Glue the second lid on top of the slats and to the PVC pipe.
7. When the glue has thoroughly bonded, put the dowelling through the center of the pipe and move the contraption to a water table, sink or outdoor space.
8. Place the dowelling ends on top of two pails or large tin cans and secure with tape or hold in a stable position.
9. Position a water source directly above the waterwheel.
10. Watch the wheel go around.

Try This:

- Move water. Place a small pail where it can be filled by the wheel, and watch the water move from the hose to the pail.

* Caution: Be careful when cutting wood pieces.

Challenge:

Design a boat that is powered by the "waterwheel."

Cork Rocket

K-3

Pneumatics at work!

Materials:

wet tissue paper
plastic bottle with small opening

Process:

1. Wet the tissue paper and shape it into a cork rocket.
2. Plug the top of the bottle with the cork rocket.
3. Squeeze the bottle hard.
4. Observe and discuss what happened. Why did the cork fly out? What happened to the air inside the bottle? What happened when the air was compressed too much?

Try This:

- Measure how far the cork flies.
- Discuss why the cork didn't continue to rocket through the air. What force slowed the rocket down? What would happen if you sent this rocket sailing off into space where there is no gravity?
- Pour 1/8 cup (30 ml) of baking soda into the bottle. Add 1/2 cup (120 ml) vinegar. Cork it quickly and watch the rocket!

Challenge:

How can you make the cork go faster? Can you invent a method to measure how fast the cork is travelling? Provide a stopwatch and measuring device.

Name ______________________________

Harness the Wind!

1. Cut on the dotted lines
2. Fold A, B, C and D into the center dot.
3. Put a fastener or a pin through the center.
4. Attach the wheel to a plastic balloon stick, pencil or wooden dowel using a pin or fastener.
5. Blow on it or hold it into the wind and watch it go!

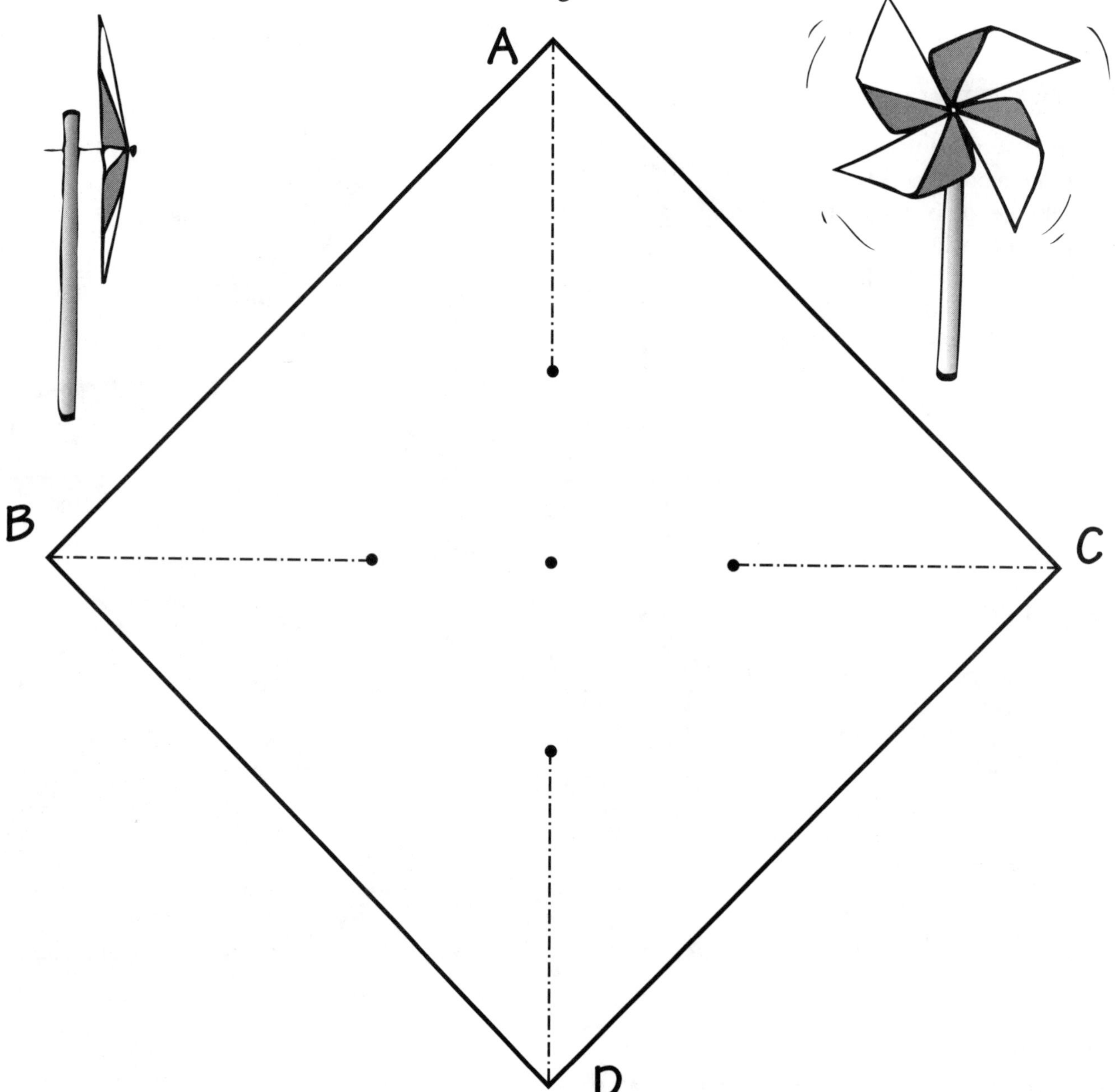

- *Leonardo da Vinci was the first person to make windmill blades turn from an internal source of power. He speculated that a windmill in reverse could be useful. From the windmill, Da Vinci invented the helicopter in the 1400s. Five hundred years later, in 1919, a working helicopter was finally built.*

Hovercraft

2-3 

A wind-powered wonder.

Materials:

sturdy cardboard
darning needle
compass
balloon
plastic tubing wide enough for neck of a balloon to fit tightly over
cool glue gun and glue sticks

Process:

1. Cut a circle out of the cardboard about 4" (10.16 cm) across. Do not let the cardboard get crumpled or bent.
2. Make a small hole in the center with the needle.
3. Glue a 2" (5.08 cm) section of tubing above the hole in the card and let it dry.
4. Inflate the balloon and fit the neck over the free end of the tube.
5. Place the contraption on a smooth, flat surface and watch it float on a cushion of air.
6. Discuss how the air that is expelled from the balloon spreads out beneath the contraption and raises it above the surface. The air cushion between the table and the flat surface of the card experience very little friction and allows the contraption to move easily.

Try This:

- Learn about the hovercraft. Christopher Cockerell invented a model of the hovercraft using tin cans. It worked and in 1955 the tin can model became the hovercraft which focuses air beneath its hull so it can float over the land, snow, ice or water.
- Write a story about where you would go if you had a hovercraft.
- Discuss the merits of the hovercraft. Why do you think its use is limited?

* Caution: Be careful when using the needle, compass and glue gun.

Challenge:

Design a contraption that uses this technology.

Water Spinner

1-3   *Caution

A real motor!

Materials:

tin can with base
nail
hammer
block
2 bendy straws cut to about 3" (7.62 cm)
plasticene or bubble gum
sturdy, lightweight string
pouring container
water
water table or outdoor environment
water smock

Process:

1. Using the hammer, nail and block (held inside), make two small holes on opposite sides of the can about 1/2" (1.25 cm) from the top.
2. Thread and knot string through the holes so the can will be suspended in the air.
3. Make two holes on either side of the can about 1/2" (1.25 cm) from the base.
4. Push the straws into the holes so that the bended end protrudes from the can. Bend the ends so that both are pointing clockwise.
5. Seal the joints with plasticine or chewed bubble gum.
6. Suspend the can from the strings and place it over a water table or take it outdoors.
7. Pour water into the can and watch it spin around as water empties through the straws.
8. Discuss the pushing force caused by the water pouring from the straws.

Try This:

- Some machines are supplied with electric energy, others with fuel. What powers this contraption? Help children understand that the energy comes from flowing water.
- Provide the opportunity for students to explore at a water table with a waterwheel, hand pump, pouring containers and droppers.

* Caution: Be careful when making holes.

Challenge:

Make a contraption powered by flowing water. Provide waterproof containers and materials, a water table or outdoor environment, pouring containers and a flowing tap or hose.

- *Hydroelectricity is a form of electricity produced by the energy of flowing water.*

Electric Energy

1-3  

The simple circuit that really works!

Materials:

2 pieces plastic-coated wire at least 6" (15.24 cm) long
1.5-3.0 volt flashlight bulb
bulb holder
1.5 volt battery (AA, C or D cell)
small screwdriver
mounting board
Mac-tak™ or plasticine
tape, pipe cleaner or rubber band for mounting battery

Process:

1. Discuss places where electricity is used in our lives.
2. Put the bulb in the bulb holder.
3. Strip the wire so that the inner strands of metal are showing at both ends.
4. Attach two wire ends to the screws on the bulb holder.
5. Attach loose ends of other wires to battery and light things up.

Try This:

- What else could be used in place of the light bulb? A buzzer?
- Use the switch to send coded messages to friends.
- Look at the wire and the bulb with a magnifying glass. What do you see inside the bulb.
- Look around! Make a list of all the things that work because of electricity.
- Discuss safety issues regarding electricity. Make some posters.
- Research some of Benjamin Franklin's inventions. He was one of the first people to experiment with electricity.

* Caution: Battery power is weak compared to the electricity we use on a daily basis. Make children aware that electricity in our homes is much more powerful and extremely dangerous. Remind them to never play with electric outlets or appliances.

* Caution: Never use old batteries. Warn children to beware of split or leaking batteries.

Challenge:

Make an On/Off switch by wrapping the wire around a paper clip. Touching the paper clip to the battery will light the bulb. Devise a switch method to turn the light on and off by moving the paper clip.

- *Electricity used to light a bulb moves through the wires and bulbs all around the circuit–it is called electric current.*
- *A battery is a special device that contains electricity-producing chemicals. Alessandro Volta invented the first electric battery (the voltaic pile) in 1800.*

Chapter 4

Contraptions for Comfort

Human beings are always trying to make things a little better than they are. Many contraptions are invented to meet our basic needs for shelter, food and water, warmth and comfort.

Let's Make a Shelter

 K-3   

Materials:

large cardboard boxes
sheets of cardboard
cardboard tubes
cloth sheets
wide masking tape
scissors

Process:

1. Discuss animal and human shelters. What is their main purpose? What elements are necessary?
2. ***Challenge:*** Build a shelter that you can fit in.
3. Provide construction materials and stand back. This should be an open-ended project where children discover questions and problem solve.
4. Ask leading questions such as: "Who needs a shelter? Why? What parts might a shelter need? Why might we need something above our heads? How can we join pieces together? Can we get in and out of this shelter?"
5. Visit and enjoy one another's structures.

Try This:

- Before building their structure, have children use toy building blocks or skewers and gumdrops to build shelters for toy animals and people.
- Take another look at these houses. What could be added? Is there a window, door, curtain, paint or siding, furniture, garden, decorations, etc.? Add these.
- Take a look at interior design. Discuss home, school, color, shape, light and texture.

* Caution: Be careful using scissors on heavy cardboard.

- *A structure provides support and must be able to resist forces; it must support its own weight as well as other weights it is designed to support.*

Caught in the Rain

 K-3   

Materials:

school backpack
papers
tape
book
plastic garbage bag

Process:

1. Provide each group with a school backpack to investigate.
2. Set up a role-playing situation in which children are walking home from school and get caught in a rainstorm.
3. ***Challenge:*** Use the items in your backpack to help keep you dry.
4. Allow children to use the backpack and items within it any way possible to keep themselves dry.
5. After the "rain," share ideas about how items were used.

Try This:

- Supply materials to make a new improved umbrella.
- Test various materials in a water table. What materials would keep you dry in a rainstorm?
- Have students sit in a circle to "create a rainstorm." The leader take the group through a series of actions: blow gently (wind), tap fingers together (the first raindrops), clap hands (heavy rain), stamp feet (thunder). Each child copies what the person to their right is doing.

* Caution: Be careful with plastic bag.

- *In the thirteenth century, South American Indians used rubber sap to waterproof clothing.*
- *The first raincoat was invented by Scottish chemist, Charles Macintosh in 1823. A layer of rubber between two pieces of wool cloth became a waterproof fabric that was made into the famous macintosh raincoat.*

Shoe-for-All

 K-3  

Materials:

collection of interesting shoes and boots
assorted interesting materials and fabrics
scissors
cool glue gun and glue sticks
adhesive tape

Process:

1. Set up shoe centers with a variety of shoes and materials at each.
2. ***Challenge:*** Interesting characters are in need of footwear. Design and make a shoe just for them. Consider a ballerina on a muddy stage, an alien on a planet covered with rubber, an astronaut who keeps floating off the moon or a child who must jump over small streams to get to school.
3. Allow children the opportunity to create footwear for the various characters.
4. Children present their shoe and its attributes.
5. Children take a critical look at each other's shoes and discuss.

Try This:

- Create a Shoe-for-All display. Label each shoe.
- Allow children to invent their own unusual characters in need of footwear.
- Children can create the perfect shoe for a parent or friend for Mother's Day, Father's Day or a birthday. The shoe will be a reflection of the individual's personality, interests and needs.
- Encourage children to experiment with various materials, tools and equipment as they create.
- Incorporate this activity with language arts and design shoes for characters in a book.

* Caution: Be careful when using the glue gun.

- *A 20-year-old cloth seller in New York was attracted by the Gold Rush of 1848. He took a few bolts of cloth to sell on the journey west, and sold all but a roll of canvas. No one wanted clothes made out of canvas, but it turned out that "up in the diggin's" where the miners worked, pants wore out very quickly. Levi Strauss made some pairs of canvas trousers to sell to miners. It wasn't long before he forgot all about gold digging–he called his pants Levi's, and they were popular with miners and cowboys. Today they are popular with everyone around the globe.*

Creative Hinges

 1-3  

Materials:

small cardboard box
scissors
adhesive tape
string
paper fasteners
single-hole punch
pipe cleaners
leather
eye screws

Process:

1. Look at hinges around the school.
2. Discuss the different types of hinges.
3. ***Challenge:*** Design your own unique hinge for a door or window on the structure.
4. Provide the materials and facilitate learning where possible.
5. Observe one another's hinges and discuss the merits and problems of each.

Try This:

- Start a hinge collection in your classroom.
- Have a Hinge Hunt throughout the school. How many hinges can you find?

- *The earliest-known metal hinges were found in Tutankhamun's tomb dating from 1350 B.C.*

Hand Warmers

 K-3  

Materials:

felt, cotton, fur, fleece
pieces of fluffy imitation fur
wire
scissors
glue
needle and thread
warm potatoes or boiled eggs
plastic containers holding warm water

Process:

1. ***Challenge:*** Invent a new way to keep hands warm
2. Provide the materials and the Challenge and facilitate inventive thinking!

Try This:

- Encourage children to use their Contraptions Lab Book to plan and design their new hand warmers.
- Ask about the practicality, appearance, costs of the hand warmer.
- Integrate this activity with a winter unit.

* Caution: Be careful when using the needle.

"Fan"tastic

1-3  

Just the contraption for a hot day!

Materials:

$8^{1/2}$" x 11" (21.6 x 27.94 cm) paper per child
single-hole punch
yarn
crayons

Process:

1. Decorate paper with colorful patterns.
2. Begin with the 8" (20.32 cm) side of the paper, and fold a strip approximately 1" (2.54 cm) wide.
3. Flip the paper over and fold it back another 1" (2.54 cm)–accordion style.
4. Continue flipping the paper and folding until all of the paper is folded into creases.
5. Tape the bottom outside flaps and allow the top to expand.
6. Punch a hole in the bottom edge.
7. Thread a string through the hole and tie.
8. Use the fan to cool yourself down on a hot day.
9. Wear the fan around your wrist when not in use.

Try This:

- Make fans of various shapes and sizes.
- Ask "Where does the power come from to make this fan work?"
- Research and discuss the effects of the various cooling techniques on the environment. Make children aware of all of these factors, and then design a graph to show which cooling method children prefer.

Challenge:

Using the Creators' Corner and the Inventors' Kit, design a new method to cool people down on a hot day.

- *When Schuyler S. Wheeler invented the electric fan to cool people down, it was a most welcome advancement over the hand-held fan. What invention is replacing the electric fan today?*

Toothbrushing Timer

K-3 

Materials:

2 clear plastic bottles
duct tape
rice, popcorn kernels or mini pasta
stopwatch

Process:

1. Fill one bottle about half full of rice, popcorn kernels or mini pasta.
2. Hold the second bottle upside down, joining the necks of the bottles together.
3. Use duct tape to make a secure seal between the two bottles.
4. Turn the timer over and using the stopwatch measure how long it takes for the contents to empty into the lower bottle.
5. ***Challenge:*** Adjust the bottles and contents to take about two minutes to empty–the time recommended for proper brushing of the upper or lower set of teeth. (Flip the timer and brush the other row for the same amount of time.)
6. ***Challenge:*** Find a use for your timer. Incorporate it into another invention.

Try This:

- Make a toothbrush holder to go with your toothbrushing timer. Discuss the problems of a wet environment and germs and the need to separate brushes from one another.
- Integrate with a health theme.

Kid Chair

 2-3  

Materials:

samples or magazine photographs of many types of chairs
Inventors' Kit
Creators' Corner
skewers, toothpicks and gumdrops
PVC pipe and joints

Process:

1. ***Challenge:*** Most furniture is made to be comfortable for adults. Design a model of a chair that would be just right for kids.
2. Provide the materials and the Challenge.
3. Provide the opportunity for children to sample various kinds of chairs: children's school chair, molded and wooden chairs, swivel chair, recliner, orthopedic chair, stool, hair salon chair, beanbag chair and swinging basket chair. Provide magazine photos if the real experience isn't possible.
4. Encourage children to plan their design in their Contraptions Lab Book.
5. Provide materials and adult assistance where necessary for children to construct models of their perfect Kid Chair.

Try This:

- Ask a physiotherapist or chiropractor to visit your class to talk about chairs, body positions and potential aches and pains.
- Visit a furniture store to look at chairs.
- Design a water chair. What problems must be overcome? Make a small prototype using water-filled balloons or rubber gloves.

* Caution: Be careful when using tools and equipment.

Lights Out

 2-3  

Materials:

10' (3 m) of string
tape
light switch
door with a doorknob
chair, desk or bed leg

Process:

1. ***Challenge:*** You are an avid bookworm and want to read into the night. Design and construct a system that will turn the lights out when Mom or Dad opens the door to check on you.
2. Provide the Challenge and materials, and let children investigate possible solutions.

Try This:

- Present this as a take-home project. Students can learn to map and sketch an accurate representation of their bedrooms and the mechanism of their Lights Out contraption.
- Are there other solutions to this problem that require a different set of materials?

* Caution: String should never be attached where it could present a risk of strangulation.

Earth Care

Our comfort depends on it! Challenge children to be aware of and to solve some pressing environmental problems. Design and technology should be used to care for and use our environment in a responsible manner as the needs and problems of human beings are being addressed.

Edible Dishes

K-3

Help save the Earth with garbage-free food.

Materials:

lettuce or cabbage leaves
crepes
waffles
pastry dough
rolling pin
scooped out fruit or vegetables (tomatoes, mushrooms, melons, etc.)
royal icing: 2 egg whites, 1/2 tsp. (2.5 ml) cream of tartar, 3 cups (720 ml) sifted icing sugar, 1 tsp. (5 ml) vanilla. Beat egg whites until frothy; add cream of tartar; beat again; gradually add icing sugar. Keep covered with a damp cloth. Makes a great cement!

Process:

1. Discuss the problems with the garbage produced by most convenience foods.
2. Brainstorm for examples of foods that do not come with excess packaging. Look for an opportunity to introduce the concept of edible dishes.
3. ***Challenge:*** Invent an edible food container.
4. Provide the materials above and the Challenge.
5. Allow children to explore with the materials and design and construct an edible food container.
6. Share these inventions with one another. Encourage discussion.

Try This:

- Set up a display of the edible dishes.
- Set up a trial of the various dishes, maybe at lunch or snack time. Ask children to evaluate the various dishes.
- ***Challenge:*** Design and make a model of a contraption that will produce your edible food containers.

- *Ice-Cream Cone: Charles Menches sold ice cream in dishes until a hot August day at the height of the Louisiana Purchase Exposition when he ran out of dishes. Ernest Hamwi was selling Middle Eastern Zalabia, a crisp wafer-like pastry sold with syrup. Menches rolled up Zalabia, scooped his ice cream on top and ice-cream cones were born!*

Recycling Center

Materials:

Inventors' Kit and Creators' Corner
large containers
plastic or wood pieces for dividers

Process:

1. Discuss problems with recycling in the home, school, workplace, mall or local restaurant.
2. Brainstorm for solutions to some of the problems with storage and cleanliness of the various recycled materials. Discuss the need to separate particular materials, the space requirements of some materials, the problems with removing staples and the cleaning of containers.
3. ***Challenge:*** Design and construct a working model of a recycling center that could be used in any home.
4. Provide materials and assistance to enable children to construct a solution to a real-life problem.

Try This:

- Look at various existing methods of storage of recyclables.
- Collect food packaging from all students for one week–the mountain of excess packaging will be an eye-opener that illustrates a need in our society.

* Caution: Be careful when using tools.

Compost Creature

2-3 

Reduce your garbage and feed your garden!

Materials:

rotting organic materials
soil
various wood, plastic or wire containers, large drums, barrels or snow fencing

Process:

1. Discuss the benefits of saving organic material.
2. Talk about the problems of saving organic material.
3. Brainstorm together to find some possible solutions to this real-life problem.
4. ***Challenge:*** Invent a Compost Creature that turns food scraps into rich organic fertilizer.
5. Encourage students to think about appearance, space requirements and potential odors or rodent attraction.
6. Test the various models in your school throughout the year. Fill the container with grass cuttings, food scraps, wood ashes, dead leaves or any other organic material you can find. (Avoid meat, dairy products and the insides of the egg.) Watch the materials disintegrate into fine, soil particles rich in the elements needed for plant growth.

Try This:

- Invite a gardener to your class to discuss various methods of composting and the benefits to the lawn, garden and produce.
- Invite a waste management representative from your neighborhood to discuss the benefits of reducing the amount of garbage you send to the curb.
- Begin this project on Earth Day.
- Invite adults to assist in the making of various composters.
- Raise funds for school activities or to donate to an environmental cause by selling this valuable composted material or by constructing and selling the composters.

Chapter 5

Communication Contraptions

Let's Communicate!

Communication is the exchange of thoughts, feelings and ideas. Humans communicate through symbols, gestures, signals, signs, the printed word, sounds and spoken words. Down through the ages a multitude of contraptions have helped us communicate better. Today we can communicate large quantities of information through various media, we can send messages all over the world very quickly, and we can talk to and see people even if they are on the other side of the world!

Communication with Sound Contraptions

We hear sounds with our ears and special equipment that can help us hear very soft sounds. People all over the world communicate many things with various kinds of sound.

Name ___________________________

Get the Message

Put a circle around each place where communication is happening in this picture.

Send a Message

1-3

Materials:

small sturdy mirrors
sunny day

Process:

1. Divide the class into partners or small groups.
2. ***Challenge:*** Send a message to your partner using a mirror and sunbeams.
3. Provide students with the time, space and materials to design a means to send messages.
4. Observe the groups sending messages to one another.

Try This:

- Try to crack the code and figure out the message being sent between other pairs.

Morse Code

a:	• —	j:	• — — —	s:	• • •	2:	• • — — —
b:	— • • •	k:	— • —	t:	—	3:	• • • — —
c:	— • — •	l:	• — • •	u:	• • —	4:	• • • • —
d:	— • •	m:	— —	v:	• • • —	5:	• • • • •
e:	•	n:	— •	w:	• — —	6:	— • • • •
f:	• • — •	o:	— — —	x:	— • • —	7:	— — • • •
g:	— — •	p:	• — — •	y:	— • — —	8:	— — — • •
h:	• • • •	q:	— — • —	z:	— — • •	9:	— — — — •
i:	• •	r:	• — •	1:	• — — — —	0:	— — — — —

Beginning of transmission: — • — • —
End of transmission: • — • — •
Error: • • • • • • • •

Drum

K-3    

The drum has been used in many cultures to send messages over distances, to tell stories or to express feeling.

Materials:

plastic container or tin can with one open end (tomato juice can works great)
1 large balloon
scissors
rubber band
small dowel, pencil or stick

Process:

1. Using scissors, cut the bottom off of the balloon.
2. Stretch the balloon tightly over the top of the tub or tin, if necessary put a rubber band around the rim to secure the balloon.
3. Use a tree twig, craft stick, piece of dowelling or pencil to beat on the drum.

Try This:

- Discuss the drum as an early form of long distance communication.
- To make the balloon easier to stretch, blow it up and let the air out prior to using it.
- Use different sized containers to create a whole drum set.
- Decorate the container with paints, stickers or wound cord prior to putting the balloon in place.
- Ask children to think about how the sound is made. How can the sound be altered?
- Encourage children to make and listen to a variety of sounds using their voices, their bodies and a variety of instruments and creative materials. Talk about the vibrations experienced, the pitch, the quality and the loudness of various sounds.
- Look around for scraps to make other instruments you can bang, scrape, tap, shake or blow.

* Caution: Be careful when using scissors.
* Caution: Do not put balloons in mouth.

Water Xylophone

1-3  

Materials:

8 small glass jars
water
food coloring (optional)
pouring container with spout (measuring cup, pitcher)
tapping device such as a small spoon, metal rod, knitting needle

Process:

1. Place the glass jars in a line.
2. Mix food coloring with water in a pouring container for visual effect.
3. Fill the first jar to the top with water.
4. Put a little less in the second jar, less again in the third and so on to the eighth jar.
5. Gently tap each jar and listen to the note it makes.

Try This:

- Ask children to describe how each of the sounds makes them feel.
- Does music communicate something? Look at music around the world and the messages and feelings it conveys.
- Incorporate this activity into your music curriculum. Study the xylophone, piano and other instruments.

* Caution: Be careful using glass jars.

Challenge:

Produce the musical scale using your water xylophone. If necessary, lead children to understand that removing and adding water will alter the sound. Can you play "Do-Re-Mi" or a simple tune?

String Phone

2-3    

Children will discover that sound waves can travel along a material.

Materials:

2 clean, dry, empty tin cans with sealable lids removed (baby formula or coffee tins)
25 m fine string
bradawl and hammer

Process:

1. With assistance, have children punch a hole in the middle of the base of each can.
2. Push one end of the string into the bottom of one can and tie a large knot.
3. Fix the other end of the string into the second can in the same way.
4. Children form partners.
5. Take the telephone outdoors and ask one partner to walk away with one can until the string is pulled taut.
6. One child speaks into their can while the other listens into the open end of their can.
7. Children take turns sending messages back and forth to one another.
8. Help children to understand that their voice causes vibrations in the string. These vibrations travel along the string to the other can where they are picked up by a partner's ear.

Try This:

- Pluck the string. What kind of noise is made?
- Study the evolution of the telephone. Set up a display of early to recent telephones. Discuss how inventions have improved upon existing technology.
- Develop communication skills, by having students make phone calls.

* Caution: Be careful when making holes.

Challenge:

Improve the telephone! Design a telephone set that is better than the existing product.

Make a three-party string phone.

- *Alexander Graham Bell (1847-1922) worked with deaf people. His understanding of how the ear works led to his invention of a device that allowed speech to travel down a wire–that device was the telephone.*
- *In 1837 Samuel Morse invented the electric telegraph which sent messages by transmitting electrical pulses along a wire. His telegraph lines spanned the U.S. He then developed the famous Morse code, a system of dots and dashes, that allowed long and short electric signals to be translated into letters of the alphabet. His code has since been simplified but is still in use, especially in ship to shore communication. (See the Morse code on page 46.)*
- *Guglielmo Marconi, an Italian physicist and electrical engineer, invented the wireless telegraph, the radio and sent the first radio signal across the Atlantic in 1901.*

Design a Better Writing Contraption

 1-3  

Materials:

samples of various writing instruments (pens, pencils, chalk, charcoal, markers, etc.)
paper
rubber bands
dowelling
straws
chalk
ink refill for ballpoint pens
thin markers

Process:

1. ***Challenge:*** Design a better writing contraption.
2. Provide children with the Challenge and the materials above.
3. Observe and assist where needed. Encourage students to think about shape, practicality, cost, convenience, appearance, shortcomings and limitations.

Try This:

- Investigate the various writing instruments down through the ages and around the modern world.
- Learn about Laszlo Biro (Ladislo Biro) (1900-1985) and the ballpoint pen, called the Biro in Europe. Biro invented the tiny metal ball tip for the pen and the ballpoint pen was invented. It was popular with British and American troops in WWII as it didn't leak with the changes in air pressure at high altitudes.
- Look at the invention of H.L. Lipmanh of Philadelphia, Pennsylvania. In 1858, he invented the popular pencil with a groove for rubber on the top.

Printing Press

2-3  

Materials:

potatoes
craft knife
paint
bowl
paper

Process:

1. Cut a potato in half.
2. Cut away part of the flat inside of the potato leaving a raised shape, letter or picture.
3. Pour paint onto a flat surface.
4. Press the flat of the potato into the paint.
5. Blot the painted surface once on a "blotter" paper.
6. Stamp the paper to be used, and your printing press is in business!

Try This:

- Using your printing press, make writing paper or wrapping paper.
- Study Johann Gutenberg (1397-1468) who pioneered printing with movable type or metal letters. In the early 1450s, he engraved mirror-image letters on blocks of metal, cast the letters in molds, cut them to shape and prepared them for printing. With the development of printing in Europe came thousands of books aiding the spread of ideas through the Western world from the fourteenth to sixteenth centuries. Gutenberg's method of printing stayed largely unchanged until the late twentieth century.

* Caution: Be careful when using the craft knife.

Challenge:

Devise a method to allow for continuous printing. Consider the use of a paint roller and small shapes or string.

Remote Control

 1-3   

Materials:

remote control for television or stereo
television or stereo which uses remote control
various tin plates and pans
large space

Process:

1. ***Challenge:*** Using the remote control, turn on your television from another room.
2. Discuss how the remote control works. It sends an invisible, infrared modulated light signal from the hand unit through the air to the control panel.
3. Provide the materials and the Challenge. Allow children to experiment with various angles to bounce signals off of the pie plates and around corners.
4. Turn on the television or stereo from around the corner!

Try This:

- Discuss ways that this kind of technology could and does make life easier. (Emergency vehicles ability to control traffic lights, start your car from inside your house on a cold day, turn lights on or off from your bed, etc.)

Warning Alarm

 K-3  

Materials:

tin cans
bells
string
Optional: materials for electrical circuit (see page 185)

Process:

1. ***Challenge:*** Design and construct a contraption that will announce the arrival of an intruder into your home, clubhouse, fort or classroom.
2. Provide materials and the Challenge and allow children to investigate, design, plan and produce their own unique alarm.

Try This:

- Discuss other uses for intruder warning contraptions.
- Add an electrical component to your alarm using the electrical circuit (see page 185).

Stethoscope

K-3   

Listen to your heart!

Materials:

3 18" (45.72 cm) pieces of plastic or rubber tubing
glass Y tube
3 tiny metal funnels
3-ring binder or duotang
paper

Process:

1. Attach one end of each piece of tubing to the ends of the glass Y tube.
2. Attach the funnels to the other ends of the tubing.
3. Hold two funnels over your ears and the third funnel on a friend's chest.
4. Listen for the heartbeat.

Try This:

- For a clearer heartbeat, place the funnel on bare skin directly over the heart.
- How many heartbeats can you hear per minute?
- How can you alter a person's heartbeat?

Just for Fun

Contraptions, Toys and Other Neat Kid Stuff

The Great Toy Challenge

K-3

Materials:

Inventors' Kit
Creators' Corner
toy box of toys

Process:

1. Provide the Inventors' Kit and the Creators' Corner.
2. ***Challenge:*** Children are getting tired of the same old toys. Santa has asked you to design and build an exciting new toy. Can you help him? Can you invent a toy that has never been played with before?
3. Inspire children by providing a toy box of invented toys.
4. Facilitate learning with comments such as: "What a great idea! How can we make that? What could children do with that toy? How could we make this toy safe enough for young children?"
5. Present toys to one another and have a play session. Encourage discussion of the toys.

Try This:

- Make a display of the toys.
- Try to identify various types of machines evident within each toy.
- Set up a toy shop center. Allow children to design and build toys over a period of days or weeks.

- *Not all inventions help us with our work–some of the greatest inventions bring fun or entertainment to our lives.*
- *The jigsaw puzzle was invented by John Spilsbury to help his students learn geography. He glued a printed map of England and Wales to a piece of wood and then cut the map into pieces using a jigsaw.*

The Matching Contraption

2-3     

A great opportunity to turn knowledge into a game!

Materials:

sturdy cardboard
paper fasteners
2 3"-5" (7.62 x 12.7 cm) thin pieces dowelling
tape
wire
1.5 volt battery (AA, C or D cell)
1.5-3.0 volt flash-light battery
light bulb
bulb holder

Process:

1. Draw one column down the left and right side of the board.
2. Punch or mark a row with an equal number of holes down each column.
3. Attach a paper fastener in each hole.
4. In one column, draw one picture beside each paper fastener.
5. In the other column, print the word to identify each picture beside each fastener. Do not print the word in the position directly opposite the picture.
6. On the back of the cardboard, wrap the bare ends of the wire around the paper fasteners to connect each word to the corresponding picture.
7. Connect a wire from one terminal of the battery to one screw on the bulb holder.
8. Connect a long wire from the other screw on the light bulb holder to a dowel. Tape the wire to the dowel with a small section of wire exposed at the end of the dowel so it acts like a pointer or wand. Touch the dowels together to test the circuit.
9. Attach one end of the third wire to the battery terminal and the other end to the other dowel.
10. Touch one dowel to a paper fastener in one column, and the other dowel to a paper fastener in the other column. The appropriate picture to word match will allow the bulb to light up.

* Caution: Be careful using the battery.

Challenge:

Create a learn-to-read game or activity.

Reinforce math, reading, environmental studies, music theory or other knowledge with this matching contraption.

Have a Ball!

 K-3  

Materials:

rubber bands
aluminum foil
clothing scraps
old sock
needle and thread
samples of different types of balls

Process:

1. Explore the materials and the display of balls.
2. ***Challenge:*** You have forgotten to bring a ball on a picnic. All you have is this box of materials. Make a ball that children can play with.
3. Provide the materials, the Challenge and help children to crumple foil into a ball and wrap it in rubber bands for bounce; roll cloth and cover in rubber bands for bounce; stuff an old sock with rubber bands, cloth or foil and sew the ends. Praise inventive ideas.
4. Play catch, "basketball," wall ball, monkey in the middle or juggle.

Try This:

- Attach "tails" of various materials to the balls.
- Invent some new games to play with your kid-made balls. Teach the games to other children in the school yard. Host a Game Day.
- Study pioneer children and the kinds of balls they used.
- Learn about James Naismith, the Canadian who saw the need for an indoor team sport that combined excitement and skill. In 1891, he invented the game that came to be known as basketball!

Rock-a-Bye Baby

 1-3  

Help the baby get back to sleep!

Materials:

berry basket or cardboard box
plastic pop bottle cut lengthwise
sturdy cardboard
balsa wood
craft wire for canopy
fabric for canopy and/or bedding
scissors
wire snips
craft knife
pencil
ruler or other measuring device
all-purpose glue, cool glue gun and glue sticks, wood glue
doll

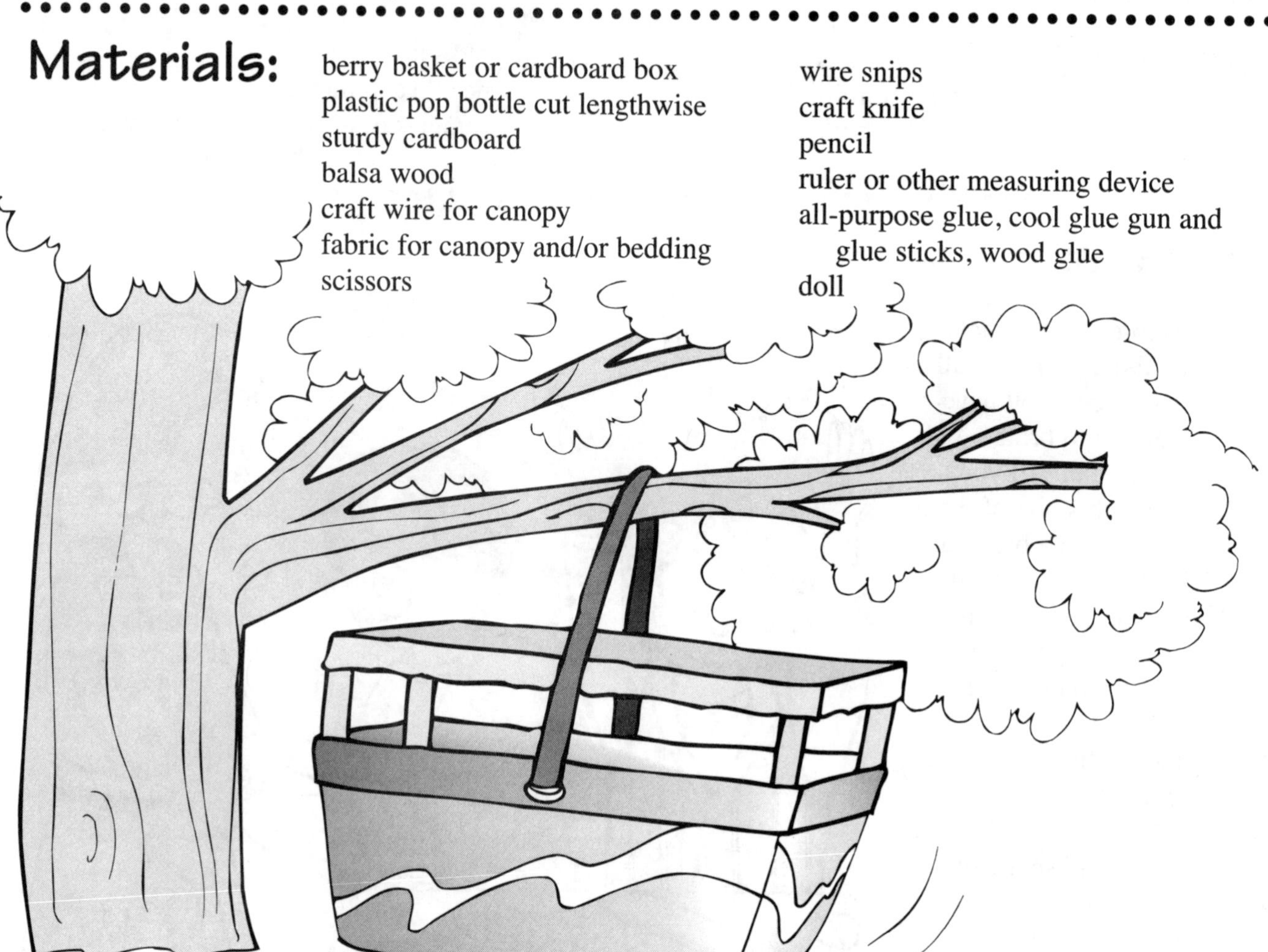

Process:

1. ***Challenge:*** The wind blew, the cradle rocked and now you need a new one for the baby doll! Using the materials on hand, make a new cradle that rocks, so the baby can get back to sleep.
2. Allow children to choose the materials they feel most comfortable working with to make a simple or elaborate cradle.

Try This:

- Decorate the cradles and set up a nursery in the house center.
- Give the cradles as gifts to siblings, grandparents or needy children at Christmastime.
- Discuss the rocking ability of the various cradles. What makes some rock better than others?

* Caution: Be careful when using the craft knife and glue gun.

Balloon Power

1-3  

Materials:

long string
hook on wall
2 large sturdy straws
long, thin balloon
tape

Process:

1. Tie a long length of string to a hook on the wall or ceiling.
2. Pull the end of the balloon over the end of one straw and tape firmly in place.
3. Tape the two straws side by side, with the ends slightly staggered so you can blow up the balloon through one of the straws.
4. Blow up the balloon, but do not tie it off. Hold the neck of the balloon so the air does not escape.
5. While holding the neck of the balloon, have a friend thread the string through the straw that does not have the balloon on one end. Thread it so the inflated balloon faces away from the free end of string.
6. Release the balloon and watch the straws be propelled along the length of the string.
7. Discuss what happens as the balloon deflates. Why is the air expelled? What effect does it have? Talk about how the air is forced from the exhaust of a jet engine in much the same way, pushing the jet forward.

Try This:

- Discuss compression. If something is compressed or squished together by force, it will store energy that can be used later to propel something.
- For a simple demonstration of the same principle, have students blow up balloons and let them go.

Challenge:

Can you reduce the friction between the straw and the string? Which works best, a taut string or a loose droopy string?

Reach Extender

Materials:

dowelling
glove
rubber band
soft stuffing (rags or quilting batting)

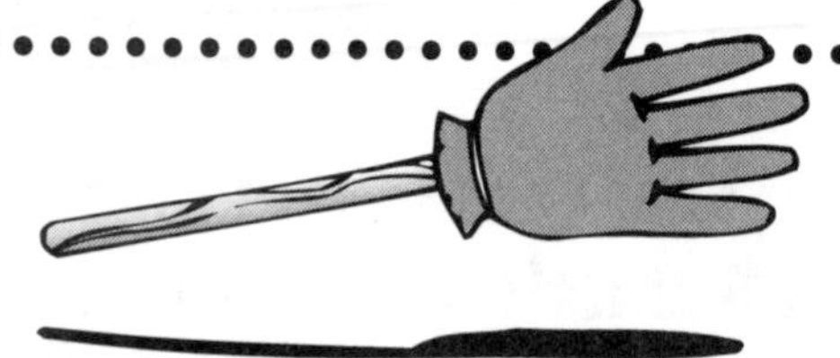

Process:

1. Stuff the glove with the filling material until it looks like a hand.
2. Attach the rubber band around the base of the glove.
3. Slip one end of the dowelling in the middle of the elastic.
4. Slide the elastic down over the glove and the dowelling to secure the glove in place.
5. Reach for things you couldn't get before.

Try This:

- Wave to your friends over a high fence or tap them on the shoulder from a distance.
- Dust the ceilings in your house.

Challenge:

Invent a method for moving the fingers of the glove.

Meals on Wheels

K-3   

Materials:

10 to 15 marbles the same size
Mason jar or other large lid
tape or glue
sturdy paper plate
set of compasses

Process:

1. Use the compass to help you find the center of the plate, and mark the bottom of the plate.
2. Glue the jar lid onto the marked center.
3. Put marbles under the lid.
4. Put snacks or a dinner on the plate and pass it around!

Try This:

- See what happens when marbles are added or removed from the lid.

Challenge:

Invent a game using the rolling (or spinning) plate.

Hand Torch

Materials:

take-apart flashlight
materials to make a circuit (see "Electricity Energy," page 32)
Inventors' Kit
Creators' Corner

Process:

1. Provide the opportunity for children to take a flashlight apart and investigate. Can they find the circuit?
2. ***Challenge:*** Design a flash-light that would be fun for a kid to use.
3. Provide the Challenge and materials and be ready with information or guidance.

Try This:

- Provide research materials that allow children to find out more about the first hand torch, later known as the flashlight. (Russian Conrad Hubert modified a friend's light-up flower invention to make a novelty electric hand torch that made him a millionaire!)

Clompers

1-3  

Materials:

2 tin cans the same size
2 lengths of fine rope or sturdy string (approx. 5' [1.5 m] long)
hammer, bradawl (or nail) and wood block

Process:

1. Turn the tins upside down and mark a spot on either side of the tin just below the top ridge.
2. Using the wood block, hammer and nail, make holes on the marks.
3. Thread one rope through each can and tie the ends off.
4. Put your feet on top of the tins and hold the ropes–one in each hand.
5. Try clomping around!

Try This:

- Dance to music or play Follow the Leader while wearing your clompers.
- Recycle old jump ropes for the rope.
- Make your clomper footprints look like animal tracks by attaching modeling clay or other printmaking material.

* Caution: Be careful using the hammer and bradawl.

Challenge:

Clompers will slip on ice. Design a way to keep them from slipping.

Invent a way to attach them to your shoes so you won't have to hold the strings.

Someone is after you. Can you use your clompers to throw them off your track?

Water Wonder

 1-3  

Make a contraption to take a message across the water.

Materials:

- corks
- rubber bands
- balsa wood
- balloon
- junior saw
- plastic tubing
- tape
- note
- water table

Process:

1. ***Challenge:*** You live on one side of a small stream, and your friend lives on the other. You must get a note across the stream to your friend. Using the materials on hand, make a contraption that will take your note across for you.
2. Provide materials and the Challenge and observe and supervise as children develop their own contraptions.
3. Encourage students to think about powering their boat across the stream.
4. Test contraptions in the water table or small nearby stream.

Try This:

- Make watertight rafts to carry notes and the school address down a large body of water. Ask raft-finders to kindly respond to the note. Use push-pins to mark the journeys and locations of various rafts.

* Caution: Be careful using the junior saw.

Electricity in a Bottle

Bring a contraption to life using static electricity!

Materials:

clear plastic 1 liter bottle with lid
cloth (silk or wool works best)
colored tissue paper or lightweight glittery confetti
paper punch–the kind that punches out neat shapes is best! (optional)

Process:

1. Cut or punch tiny confetti-sized shapes or characters in tissue paper.
2. Pour the paper bits into the plastic container and close the lid.
3. Rub the plastic surface with the cloth. Watch the bits inside pop around as the surface gets charged with static electricity.

Try This:

- Listen.
- Remove the lid and hold the bottle upside down. Why don't the bits fall out?
- Try other things inside the bottle, like salt or sugar. Can you get them to dance?
- Rub a balloon's surface on fabric or your head until it is charged. Attach a paper nose, eyes, mouth and some crazy hair.

Challenge:

Your best friend is ill and must stay in bed for a long time. Design a "toy-in-a-bottle" that would be easy to play with in bed.

Resources

Evaluating a Child's Creative Thinking Progress

To evaluate creative thinking, observe children in a wide variety of activities. Focus on growth, the process of problem solving and imaginative thinking. Assess a broad base of concept and skill development using observation checklists, anecdotal comments, achievement records, creative outcomes, growth profiles and portfolios. Photographic records of contraptions make an excellent ongoing record of progress and provide a base for discussion and evaluation. Children from three to nine years of age will participate with natural enthusiasm and curiosity. They demonstrate sustained interest in creating and problem solving. Through hands-on experience they will use their senses to explore and discriminate, ask questions and express ideas freely and develop increasing language, cognitive, social and motor abilities. Watch for these particular skills.

Child three to five years of age will:

- use a trial and error method to explore physical properties of objects
- make simple casual relationships by association
- demonstrate intuitive feel for symmetry, scale and order
- manipulate materials in inventive ways
- use tools in an individual manner limited by fine and gross motor skill development
- become visually aware of detail
- experiment with form, space and movement

Child five to seven years of age will:

- demonstrate an understanding of cause and effect
- follow three-step instructions
- manipulate materials in inventive ways
- recognize similarities and differences
- develop visual awareness of shape, detail, scale, design, conservation and symmetry
- begin to make plans before carrying out an activity
- see parts or wholes but not parts in relation to wholes
- recognize symbolic forms
- demonstrate a variety of problem-solving techniques

Child seven to nine years of age will:

- demonstrate a good understanding of cause and effect
- focus on detail without losing sight of the whole
- conserve number and length
- express and receive ideas in symbolic forms
- manipulate materials in creative ways
- make use of a rich vocabulary before, during and after an activity
- manipulate tools and materials in a competent manner
- demonstrate an understanding of scale, balance, design, space detail and motion
- preplan work through discussion and sketches

Evaluation of the Child

You may wish to use this checklist several times per child during the year. Date your evaluation so you can compare and note areas of progress.

Child's name ______________ Date ______________ Does the child . . .	Never	Some-times	Always
Recognize a need that could be addressed with design and technology?			
Demonstrate initiative?			
Experiment and manipulate materials in an inventive manner?			
Use vocabulary that indicates an understanding of science and technology?			
Demonstrate the ability to organize and plan a project appropriate for age level?			
Show attention to materials, detail, practicality and scientific principle?			
Demonstrate a working knowledge of the tools needed to create?			
Make use of a variety of techniques to create and complete works?			
Demonstrate a degree of visual awareness appropriate to his age level?			
Demonstrate an increasing awareness of detail, scale, conservation, symmetry and use of space?			
Express ideas about the work verbally?			
Demonstrate insight into various activities?			
Incorporate creative thinking and problem-solving skills when creating a work?			
Demonstrate progressive skill development?			
Consolidate problem-solving skills in all areas?			
Demonstrate an understanding of the end product created?			
Work well in group projects?			
Appraise own work?			
Take pride in his work?			
Show an appreciation of classmates' efforts and differences?			
Complete given tasks?			
Demonstrate a sustained interest and enthusiasm in activities?			

Scavenger Lists

Where Can I Find Free Materials?

Seek out the best spots in your community to scavenge great materials. Send a letter home with students that lists the kinds of materials your classroom could use, and you will tap into a valuable resource. Enlist the help of local businesses, express an interest in excess materials, samples, donations or some valuable trash.

Check out your local resources with the eye of a scavenger! Here are a few suggestions.

hardware store
art supply store
local newspaper office
framing shop
electronics shop
small equipment repair shop
recycling center
woodworking shop
building site
auto repair shop
garden center
thrift shop
fast food restaurant
grocery store
textiles company
office supply store
computer shop
craft supply store
floral shop
electrician's business
waste management facility
lumberyard
old toolboxes
students' homes and attics
clothing manufacturer
garage sales
airline company
moving company
flooring company

Try This:

- Provide shopkeepers and business owners with a large box that has your name on it, and ask them to save interesting scraps for you. Pick up your box once a month.
- *Where do you keep all this junk?* Make storage easier by sorting materials into boxes. Materials should be readily visible and attainable by students.
- Cut, shape, fold, crumple or combine particular materials to stimulate inventive thoughts.
- If you can't find what you need, make it.

Materials Worth Scavenging

ball bearings
magnets
clock workings
metal ruler
specialized glues
small vise
computer chips
discarded computer equipment
discarded appliances and utensils
discarded toys
various kinds of tape
balsa wood
large and small buttons
corks
metal washers
clothespins
beads and beans
wire
ribbons and shoelaces
rubber scraps
jar seals
reusable containers
pipe cleaners
craft sticks
cartons and boxes of all shapes and sizes
Plasticine™ and clays
paper clips and fasteners
polystyrene packing peanuts and trays
tin trays, pans and cans
coat hangers
carpets and flooring scraps
thread spools
plastic bottles
wheels from toys, skates, bicycles
plastic tubing
broom handles and dowels
discarded tools
kitchen cutting board
computer disks
segments of rubber hose
electronic components
old telephones
old jewelry
old running shoes
wood scraps
fabric scraps with interesting textures
toothpicks and skewer sticks
screw hooks and eyes
paintbrushes
coins and keys
string, yarn, twine and thread, waxed floss
sealable plastic bags
wallpaper sample books
balloons
rubber bands and elastic string
frame shop mat scraps
cardboard
paper rolls and cups
foam balls
safety pins
bubble wrap
foil wrap
straws
edibles: marshmallows, gumdrops
thumbtacks
matchboxes

Basic Skills for Making Working Models

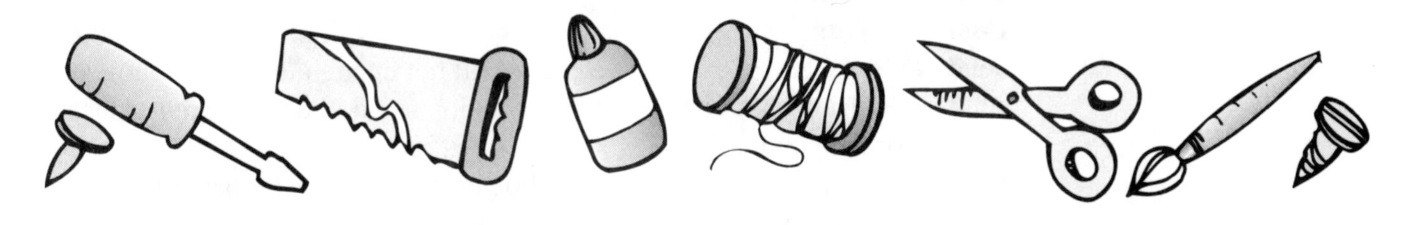

Planning

How do you turn an idea into a working model? Help children explore this question. Provide opportunities for children to plan, discuss, assess materials and equipment available, sketch and measure, make a design plan, make lists and invite assistants.

Measuring: Provide instruction and equipment for measuring and marking before making holes, shaping or cutting.
Measure twice; cut once!

Using Tools and Equipment

An important part of turning ideas into contraptions is learning to plan and use tools and materials properly. Safety guidelines should be made clear to children. Caution and supervision is required when using all tools.

Cutting and Shaping Using Sharp Tools

Sharp tools are dangerous! Supervision is essential!

Scissors: Scissors should be used for cutting cardboard, paper and other light materials. They are the safest cutting tool. Keep closed when not in use; work with the tips facing away from the body. Adult supervision may be required for the cutting of heavy materials.
Knives: Kitchen knives will work for some projects. A sharp craft knife may be used for cutting soft wood. Cut one section at a time, with a smooth, steady motion, blade facing away from you, on a flat, firm surface. Straight lines can be cut against a metal ruler. Always keep fingers away from the blade.
Junior Saw: A junior saw can be used for cutting materials that cannot be cut by scissors. Adult supervision is essential. Mark the cutline with pencil. Put the material to be cut in a small table vise, C-clamp or bench hook, or have it held firmly in place. Use a flat, sturdy work surface.

Joining and Connecting

A **spirit level** will show you if the materials are joined straight and level.
Glues: Glues join most material easily. White glue or carpenter's glue will work for most projects. Avoid glues containing cyanoacrylate, fungicides or those with harmful vapors.
Cool Glue Gun: A cool glue gun with glue sticks will provide a fast, sturdy bond. Despite its name, this glue gun is still hot enough to cause a burn, and adult supervision should be provided. Caution should be taken not to touch the glue or the gun until cool.
Connecting: Paper, cardboard and fabric can be joined with paper fasteners, staples, tape, tacks or Velcro™ .
Needle and Thread: Supervision should be provided. A needle threader will be helpful.
Hammering: Large sturdy pieces of wood can be nailed together. Use junior hammers and ensure that the heads are firmly attached to the shafts. For safe hammering, push the nail into a scrap cardboard holder, and hold the cardboard while hammering the nail or predrill the hole with a very small drill bit.

Making Holes

Holes should be marked before punching or drilling.

Punch: A single-hole paper or leather punch will work well on many light-weight materials, paper, leather, fabric, cardboard and some plastics.
Bradawl, Center Punch or Knitting Needle: Mark the position and poke the hole. Work over a thick piece of polystyrene, soft scraps of wood or cutting board to prevent injury and damage to surfaces. Use different thickness for different size holes.
Hand Drill: Holes may be started with the bradawl or knitting needle or center punch before drilling. Drill on a flat, soft, surface such as a layer of polystyrene or similar material. Materials to be drilled can be held in a vise or C-clamp. Tie back long hair, necklaces or other materials that could get caught in the drill; replace blunt drill bits; supply goggles if children will be near the drilling action and keep fingers away from exposed gears.

Finishing

Smoothing: A surface can be smoothed or sharp edges rounded with a file or sandpaper. A sanding block will make sanding flat surfaces quick and easy. Wrap a block of wood with sandpaper and fastened paper edges on the back. Inexpensive commercially made blocks can be obtained from hardware or building stores.
Covering with Paint, Stains and Varnishes: Apply paint with a brush, stain with a wide brush or cloth and varnish with a wide brush. Read contents of container carefully. Wear old clothing as it will surely get a spot somewhere.

Encourage respect and proper care for all tools and equipment.

The Great Invention Convention

Host an Invention Convention to inspire creative ideas and to provide a forum for sharing inventions.

Display Categories

Inventions that make life easier.
Inventions that make life better.
Inventions that make life more fun.

Set up your Invention Convention as a competition or a cooperative sharing of inventive ideas. Display the inventions in the gymnasium or library.

Prepare for the Convention

Lead up to your event with a study of important inventions, a look at famous inventors and a visit from a local inventor.

Share the Excitement!

Invite parents, friends, members of local businesses, students from other schools, politicians and other community members who will recognize students' achievements.

Get Coverage

Invite the local media to cover your event.

Invention Station

Have one group of students research and present information on some well-known inventions. Participants may visit this station to learn about popular inventions.

Name That Invention

Set up a table with obscure inventions. Participants guess what they think each item might be. Record answers and provide a prize for a student who names all of the items.

Meet Benjamin Franklin

One group of children is designated to role-play. Each child is assigned an inventor to study and take on the character of. These inventors mingle throughout the convention, answering questions about their lives and inventions.

Provide Convention Challenges

Turn a Box Inside Out: Take a box apart, then put it back together with the inside on the outside. Provide boxes, scissors and tape or glue.
Take Apart Challenge: Take an object apart. Provide screwdrivers; pliers; tweezers; a variety of take-apart items such as clocks, motors, radios, cassette players . . . .
Design a Better Playground: Make a model of a better playground. Provide straws, toothpicks, skewers, discs, wooden shapes, plasticine, marshmallows, string, and tape.

Contraptions Bibliography

Ardley, Neil. *Dictionary of Science*. Dorling Kindersley Limited, Raincoast Books, Vancouver, 1994.

Bender, Lionel. *Invention*. Eyewitness Books, Dorling Kindersley Limited, Stoddart Publishing Co., Canada, 1991. Also available in U.S. through Houghton Mifflin Company, Boston.

Carletti, Silvana, Suzanne Girard, and Kathlene Willing. *Sign Out Science: Simple Hands-On Experiments Using Everyday Materials*. Markham, ON: Pembroke Publishers Ltd., 1993.

Carpenter, Thomas. *Inventors: Profiles in Canadian Genius*. Camden House Publishing/Telemedia Publishing Inc./Firefly Books, 250 Sparks Avenue, Willowdale, Canada, 1990.

Clements, Gillian. *The Picture History of Great Inventors*. Alfred A. Knopf, New York, 1994.

Kydd, G., and Ricki Wortzman. *Explorations in Science*. Addison Wesley, 1992.

Lowery, Lawrence. *The Everyday Science Sourcebook: Ideas for Teaching in the Elementary and Middle School*. University of California, Berkeley, Dale Seymour Publications, 1985.

Macaualay, David. *The Way Things Work*. Houghton Mifflin Company, Boston, 1988.

Newton, Doug and Lynn. *Design and Technology* (Bright Ideas Series). Scholastic, 1990.

Norris, Doreen, and Joyce Boucher. *Observing Children in the Formative Years*. The Board of Education for the City of Toronto, Toronto, 1989.

Richards, R. *An Early Start to Technology*. Simon & Schuster, Toronto, 1990.

Richardson, Robert. *The Weird and Wondrous World of Patents*. Sterling Publishing Co., Inc., New York, 1990.

Willing, K.R., and S. Girard. *Learning Together: Computer-Integrated Classrooms*. Markham, ON: Pembroke Publishers Ltd., 1990.

Wyatt, Valerie. *Inventions: An Amazing Investigation*. Owl Books/Greey de Pencier Books, Toronto, 1987.